ISBN 978-0-483-42481-4
PIBN 10759895

ENGLISH AND
AMERICAN
LITERATURE

STUDIES IN LITERARY
CRITICISM, INTER-
PRETATION AND
H I S T O R Y

By C. H. SYLVESTER

*Formerly Professor of Literature and
Pedagogy in the State Normal
School at Stevens
Point, Wis.*

INCLUDING COMPLETE
MASTERPIECES

IN TEN VOLUMES
With Numerous Halftone Illustrations
VOLUME THREE, ORATIONS

15890

CHICAGO
BELLOWS BROTHERS COMPANY
1906

Part Five

Orations

Contents

Illustrations

Illustrations

Forms of Prose Composition

Forms of Prose Composition
/5890

It seems to be generally accepted that **four** methods of expression are to be found in prose : *Narration, description, exposition* and *argumentation.* Narration deals with things in action, description with the appearance of things, exposition explains the relations ideas bear to one another, and argumentation not only does this, but tries at the same time to convince its readers. Theoretically, this distinction is very easy to make, for action is the life of narration, appearance the theme of description, explanation and exposition are synonymous, and no one argues but with the hope of convincing. What can man do more than to tell what has been done, tell how a thing looks, show how one thing follows from another or is related to it, and endeavor to bring another person to the same state of mind ?

The accuracy and completeness of the classification is most evident until one attempts to apply it practically to existing literature, and then he finds that no literary masterpiece belongs entirely to any one of the classes, **but that these mingle** and unite, one or the other usually predominating. This ruling element, the one which is proportionately greater, will govern the classification of a selection. In any story, narration and description meet at every turn and not infrequently exposition is found freely intermingled, while novels have been written with the avowed sole purpose of changing the beliefs of a people. *Uncle Tom's Cabin* is a story of intense dramatic activity, and abounds in vivid descriptions of places and persons. It is generally dealing with incidents relating to the characters of the story, yet it really makes an exposition of the evils of slavery, and certainly was no small factor in stirring the American people into vigorous action against the slave dealers. Yet no one would classify the book otherwise than among the narratives. Although into Burke's *Conciliation* other elements enter, yet everyone will admit it to be argumentative in the highest degree. So while it is well to classify the selections read, yet fine theoretical distinctions should be abandoned. It is not so necessary to classify and name, as it is to compare and distinguish.

The selections we have printed illustrate most excellently the four methods of expression. *The Great Stone Face*, *Wee Willie Winkie*, and *The Ambitious .Guest* are narratives, as pure as we can select. Few are finer ideal studies into human character than is the last which deals so delicately with the characteristics of the different types assembled beneath that humble roof. *The Cricket on the Hearth* and the greater part of Lamb's *Dissertation on Roast Pig* may be classed in the same category. The *Roger de Coverley* papers are descriptive, Emerson's *Self-Reliance* is in the main an exposition, while the great speeches of Webster and Burke are argumentative.

Narratives have been variously classified but a classification of them is not more satisfactory than of other forms of literature. A narrative is true or fictitious, and there appears the first principle of classification. Truthful narratives are personal when they are the simple account of the deeds of some person or thing, biographical when they show a clear and evident purpose to detail the events in the life of the person, historical when they deal with larger and more complicated questions and when the actors are as numerous as the actions are various. Fictitious narratives comprise short stories and novels. Of the latter there are many forms as has been explained elsewhere. One prominent writer notes the following types: (1) The realistic novel that is true to actual life and often enters into the discussion of important questions of record. (2) The novel of life and manners which is largely descriptive and in which the exigencies of the plot give way to the study of customs. (3) The novel of incident in which the plot is everything and description and character study are avoided or subordinated to action. (4) The romance which deals with things as they were in days long past and with actions that little concern the present. Marvelous and even supernatural incidents crowd its pages. (5) The idealistic novel which paints the world as it should be and makes its actors more nearly perfect than the world accepts as typical. (6) The novel with a purpose which seeks to convert its readers by the vividness of its portraits rather than by argument, though by means of many detailed conversations its theories are often freely discussed and fully substantiated.

Description deals with the individual and not with the class. A fine description is a work of art in its highest sense and is closely allied to painting, than which it is even more delicate and refined; for while the painter lays his color on the canvas and our eyes see the entire picture in all its minutest detail, the writer can only suggest the idea and stimulate the imagination to create for itself the picture in the mind of the artist. Yet such is the marvelous power of words when handled by a master that one can see by them almost as vividly as by the sense of sight. The reader is transported to far-away lands, strange men and animals surround him, the skies glare above him, silver lakes sparkle in the sun, brooks murmur against their fern-covered sides, and birds move the soul with their sweet music. Evening draws on, and the landscape glimmering fades away; the stars come out one by one and by and by the moon steals slowly up the sky. Peace and quiet reign over the darkened world. Neither sculpture nor painting can depict these changes; it rests with the magic of words.   But the reader must do his share.   ˌHe must give time to his reading, must yield himself gently to its influence, must not force himself into the writer's mood but must receive and accept.   Then descriptive literature will yield its keenest pleasures.

Exposition on the other hand deals with the class and is abstract.   For this very reason the demands made upon its reader are infinitely greater.   It is assumed that the concrete examples and specific instances necessary for the interpretation of the abstract are already in mind and that the barest allusion to them will be sufficient.   So exposition naturally follows narrative and description.

Successful argumentation depends upon proof and persuasion.   It is addressed to the reason or to the emotions.   Burke and Webster endeavor to establish their respective positions by irrefutable arguments.   When Beecher addressed the people on the slavery question he appealed strongly to their emotions and sought to make them act because of their intense feeling.   One characteristic of all literary masterpieces is unity, but in none is this of more importance than in the expository and argumentative types.

Studies

1. Find three descriptive passages in *The Ambitious Guest;* three in *Wee Willie Winkie.* Which story contains the greater number of descriptive passages?

2. Look for argumentative passages in *The Great Stone Face.*

3. Look for expository passages in the narratives of the first two Parts.

4. Can you find narrative in any of the essays of Parts Three and Four?

5. Select a passage from Emerson's *Self-Reliance* and set forth in logical order the steps in his exposition.

Study of an Oration

Orations

With the study of the oration we enter a new department of literature. The essay is written to be read, the oration to be heard; the essay is to please, to entertain, perhaps to instruct, sometimes to convince; the oration is to arouse the feelings, to carry conviction, to stir the public to action. It is a formal production, addressed directly to its hearers; it is in form or meaning in the second person. Even when descriptive or eulogistic it is a direct address. The orator says, "These are my opinions and here are my reasons for so thinking. Will you not accept my view and think and act accordingly?"

The oration naturally divides itself into three sections. There is an *introduction* in which the speaker clears the way, opens the question and lays down the principles he proposes to advocate, or indicates the course of his argument. The *body* follows. Here the principles are elucidated, the arguments advanced and properly established, or the descriptions elaborated and finished. The last section is the *conclusion* which may consist of a brief review or summary of the inferences drawn, or of a plea for belief and for action in accordance with the principles of the speaker.

As a final part of the conclusion there is often a paragraph or so of most eloquent diction, the peroration. It is intended to appeal particularly to the emotions of the hearers, to carry them out of themselves, to move them in spite of themselves and to leave them feeling intensely the earnestness and sincerity of the speaker.

Before the art of printing was invented, public opinion was molded almost entirely by public speaking, and for a great many years afterward the orator was the greatest of leaders. By the magic of his eloquence he changed the views of men and inspired them to deeds of greatest valor. The fiery orations of a Demosthenes, of a Cicero; the thrilling words of a Peter the Hermit or a Savonarola; the unanswerable arguments of a Burke or a Webster, have more than once turned the course of history.

But when the newspaper first found its way into the hands of thinking men the power of the orator felt the influence of its silent opponent and began to wane. To-day it is not often that multitudes are swayed by a single voice. The debates and stump-speeches of a political campaign change but few votes. The preacher no longer depends wholly upon the convincing power of his rhetoric to make his converts. The representatives of a people in a parliament or a congress speak that their words may be heard through the newspapers by their constituents more than with the expectation that their speech will carry a measure through the House they are addressing.

Yet we still listen with pleasure to a fervid speaker whose earnestness of manner carries the conviction of his sincerity, and even against our will we are moved by elegant sentences and pleasing tones. The orator will continue to be a power though in a different way. Conditions have changed and the ponderous periods and elaborate figures that characterized the orators of classic epochs are giving place to the plain, lucid diction and the simple, true-hearted tones of the modern speaker.

Shakespeare puts into the mouth of Marc Antony his famous oration over the dead body of Cæsar, and the course of a convincing argument was never more clearly seen than in the actions of that ignorant body of Roman citizens. Before an audience of nineteenth century laborers, fresh from the perusal of their daily papers in which headlines, skillfully colored reports, and able editorials have shaped or perverted their opinions, the Roman soldier would have produced no such revolution in sentiment, however much the people might have admired the skillful iteration of his "honorable men" or the masterly way in which he made prominent the good qualities of his martyred chief.

Everyone admires the oration. "I come to bury Cæsar, not to praise him." There is no

hint of ais real purpose. How readily he falls in
with the opinions of the populace loud in their
approbation of the acts of Brutus and his co-
conspirators! With what ready tongue he de-
fends their acts and praises the "honorable"
intent which led them on! Then little by little
as he has really gained the "ears" for which he
asked, with what delicate skill he lets his auditors
see his idea of the real character of Cæsar, till
the gaping wounds become indeed dumb mouths
to plead against his murderers. When the time is
fully ripe he brings forth the will, but not until
the people wrought to the highest pitch of excitement and as furious in their resentment as they
had been loud in their praise demand and insist
and virtually compel him to reveal its contents.
Then his conclusion follows with irresistible effect.
True, he was no orator as Brutus was, but a plain
man who had sounded the depths of the human
heart and learned the secrets of its action. After
all, that is oratory, and oratory of the most accomplished kind.

The true oration leads through the hearing to
conviction and to action. So the canons by which
one judges it must be different from those of any
other form of literature. The greatest speakers
have been plain men — many of them were not
highly educated, and some of them might be
called unlearned even. There are instances in
which the most polished oratory, that which

showed most conclusively the trained intellect and which was fashioned with all the art that the schools can give, has lost its power and is remembered only by the scholars who still point with pride to its literary excellence. But the burning thoughts of some less cultivated man have become the household words of a nation. The heart must go into an oration if it is to reach an audience.

No great man was simpler in his tastes, plainer in his manner, rougher in his exterior, than Abraham Lincoln. Yet as a public speaker he has had few equals. He grew up in the west. He listened to campaign speeches and read whatever he could find. His clear vision pierced to the core of a matter and he saw what was necessary to make a convincing argument. To master these essentials became his task — his pleasure. Simplicity, directness, logic, brevity, he sought and obtained. He gathered a wealth of illustration, he mastered the art of vivid presentation, he marshaled his facts in logical array, and threw his whole soul into his delivery. With this equipment he found his way into politics and entered his memorable series of debates with Stephen A. Douglas.

His success was known and appreciated in the west and his reputation traveled eastward. With no little trepidation in his own heart and some fear in the minds of his warmest supporters he finally stood before one of the largest and most cultivated audiences the city of New York could furnish, and again his convincing oratory made its way. The self-trained western lawyer outshone the most brilliant and studied orators of the great metropolis.

On the nineteenth day of November, 1863, a great assembly gathered on the battlefield of Gettysburg. It was a day of solemn dedication. A beautiful monument had been erected to those who but four months before had given up their lives to save the north from further invasion. It was an important occasion, a day of studied ceremony. Edward Everett was the orator of the day and had prepared himself with unwonted care to do honor to the dead. His oration was long, scholarly, perfect according to all the rules of his art. It was one of his greatest efforts and his hearers knew they had listened to a masterly creation. But it was forgotten when they heard a simple little address delivered by the President of the United States, Abraham Lincoln. Here is what Lincoln said:

Fourscore and seven years ago, our fathers brought forth on this continent a new nation, conceived in liberty, and dedicated to the proposition that all men are created equal. Now we are engaged in a great civil war, testing whether that nation, or any nation so conceived and so dedicated, can long endure. We are met on a great battlefield of that war. We have come to dedicate a portion of that field as a final resting-place for those who here gave their lives that that nation might live. It is altogether fitting and proper that we should do this. But in a larger sense we cannot dedicate, we cannot consecrate, we cannot hallow this ground. The brave men, living and dead, who struggled here, have consecrated it far above our poor power to add or detract. The world will little note, nor long remember, what we say here, but it can never forget what they did here. It is for us, the living, rather to be dedicated here to the unfinished work which they who fought here have thus far so nobly advanced. It is rather for us to be here dedicated to the great task remaining before us,— that from these honored dead we take increased devotion to that cause for which they gave the last full measure of devotion,— that we here highly resolve that these dead shall not have died in vain,— that this nation, under God, shall have a new birth of freedom,— and that government of the people, by the people, for the people, shall not perish from the earth.

This little address contains but ten sentences, and about two hundred seventy-five words. But see how perfect it is! Analyze the thought, sentence by sentence, and see what perfect unity characterizes it. It is difficult to make the sentences shorter or simpler, but a tabulation may help to the meaning at a single glance. The figures indicate the sentences taken in their natural order. Read the outline carefully and notice that the condensation has caused the omission of many minor thoughts.

I. INTRODUCTION.
   1. Spirit of the nation.
     (a) Conceived in liberty.
     (b) Dedicated to equality.
   2. Shall such a nation endure?
     The war will determine.
   3. Where we meet.
     A great battlefield.
   4. Why we meet.
     To dedicate.
   5. A fitting meeting.

II. BODY.
   6. Impossible, in a larger sense, to dedicate.
   7. Because the soldiers dedicated more perfectly.
   8. World's opinion of:
     (a) Our words.
     (b) The soldiers' deeds.

III. Conclusion.

9-10. Our duty:
(a) To be dedicated.
(b) To take increased devotion.
(c) To resolve:
  (1) That their deaths shall not be in vain.
  (2) That this nation shall have greater freedom.
  (3) That the people's government shall not perish.

When the thought has been mastered, consider the sentences separately, noticing their form and the words that compose them. Can redundant words be found? Can different words or phrases be substituted for the ones given here without destroying the euphony or the meaning? Is there anything in the order of arrangement of words that does not please you? In the sixth sentence compare in meaning the words *dedicate, consecrate* and *hallow*. Which is the strongest? Is the reason given sufficient to account for our inability? The eighth sentence is a noteworthy one in its perfect balance. How many sets of words are placed in opposition? What is meant by the "last full measure of devotion"? Is the expression an apt and beautiful one? What is the distinction in meaning among the three phrases, *of the people, by the people,* and *for the people?*

Is the difference in meaning sufficient to account for their use? Does the similarity in form, the apparent repetition, add to the force? Which is the best sentence, everything considered? Are the sentences arranged in order of climax, the most important and most sonorous last? How do the various sentences compare in length?

When the address has been studied by this outline, and the questions answered to the satisfaction of the reader, it will begin to be manifest why this is, in spite of its brevity, one of the world's great orations.

General Directions

In the study of an oration the student should first read it through from beginning to end. Then he should determine how much of it may be considered as introductory, what part of it is the body, and where the conclusion properly begins. This done he should prepare a careful outline of the thought in each section. In the introduction he should consider the purpose of that section and its relation to the body. His analysis of the body of the discourse should show the chief line of thought and the secondary or contributory lines. He should weigh the arguments advanced and consider for himself whether these are logical and convincing. Then he should take up the conclusion to judge whether it follows naturally and logically from the rest of the oration and whether it is convincingly stated and adds to the force of the argument. If it is a summary of facts, is it a true one and are the facts put in an effective form and arrangement so they assist in making the desired impression? The student here as elsewhere in this course should not hesitate to write the results of his own thinking and to put into his own language the thoughts of the author. Often in this attempt he convicts himself of error or clarifies the meaning of many an obscure statement. To condense into

as brief space as possible the thoughts of an oration is excellent practice. In doing this, note
how much has been put in merely for the sake of
sound. All the illustrative facts, all the figures
that add merely to the beauty or the convincing
force can be ruthlessly set aside and the barest
statement of facts alone preserved. It is sometimes
almost startling to see how much has been said for
effect and how many times the changes have been
rung on the same idea. As the speech is primarily
to be heard, much care has been given by the
author to clothing his thoughts in euphonious
words and to arranging them in effective and mel-
odious order.

In an oration repetition, which in other forms
of literature is annoying, may become a merit. For
once again it must be remembered that the oration
is to be caught by ear and the hearer cannot
ponder over everything that is said but must
hasten on to other ideas as rapidly as the speaker
utters them. Skillful repetition with attractive
variation is exceedingly effective.

The personal element is a factor of great importance. In fiction, in the essay, and in most
forms of poetry, the reader is often left in doubt
as to the real feeling, the sincere belief of the
writer. But in the oration the student has a
right to assume that the speaker is voicing his own
sentiments, is advocating the principles he intends
to follow. Often the orator brings his own per-

sonality into the foreground and here the student
will consider the purpose indicated by such a
course and whether by so doing the author has
made himself more effective, or has lessened the
force of his arguments by the very prominence he
has given himself. How much of Webster's reply
to Hayne is purely personal? What justification
has Webster for making himself the central figure
of the early pages of his debate? Does he obtrude
himself into the argument when he has once begun
upon the main question? How much of the personal element appears in the conclusion? Would
the general effect of the speech have been intensi-
fied if he had made it much less personal?

Other questions will occur to the reader. Does
the speaker confine himself closely to his argument,
or does he at times desist, perhaps introduce
something to enliven his remarks, to catch the
wavering attention of his hearers? Does he ever
rise above the special instance which he is considering and utter broad and general truths in
startling or convincing form? Can you find
single sentences which may be taken bodily from
the text and be in themselves complete and strik-
ing statements beautifully expressed?

Are there passages of unusual eloquence, and
what relation do they bear to others? Do they
follow or precede the arguments and proofs? Do
they show that the speaker has convinced himself?
Select for frequent reading a number of the pas-

sages that you admire and try to determine what constitutes their charm.

In Webster's speech, where does the peroration begin? If it were taken from the oration would it be considered eloquent and thrilling? Does it depend directly upon the preceding arguments, or does it seem like a patriotic outburst from a heart full of feeling? Read it aloud. Is it pleasing to the ear, sonorous and rhythmical? Are all the sentences well balanced? As you read do the thoughts flow smoothly and join readily as though one followed necessarily from another, and do they increase in intensity to the end? If so, this peroration is a *climax* in form as it is the climax of the speech.

As elsewhere in the course, the questions we print can be little more than suggestive. When one studies by himself he must cultivate an inquiring frame of mind, he must learn to quiz himself and to answer his questions to the satisfaction of his own reason. In this way he will eventually gain a power that no class instruction could possibly give him. He will make mistakes and form erroneous judgments, but the questioning habit will eventually convict him of his errors and he will revise his opinions till in the end he finds himself more firmly established in right views than if his correct ideas had been at first established by the ablest instructors. Besides he will have an independence of mind and clearness of thought that can be acquired in no way but by self-reliant thinking.

Daniel Webster

Among the eminent men who have influenced legislative assemblies in Great Britain and the United States, during the past hundred and twenty years, it is curious that only two have established themselves as men of the first class in English and American literature. These two men are Edmund Burke and Daniel Webster.—*E. P. Whipple.*

Daniel Webster

1782–1852

As a patriotic orator Daniel Webster will always stand the foremost American. Of commanding presence, with a courtesy and graciousness of manner that never failed to please, he secured a loyal following wherever he went, and for years was the greatest power in American politics though he was never able to secure the highest office his country had to offer.

His education was acquired under the most adverse conditions. His parents were poor and though ambitious for their son were able to assist him but little. Moreover he was delicate and often feeble and gave little promise of being the large and powerful man he became. By his own exertions and the practice of rigid economy, aided by warm personal friends and the loving care of his parents, he gained his preparatory education and was able to enter Dartmouth College at the age of fifteen. While at Exeter in preparation for college he found his greatest trouble in his public declamations. "Many a piece did I commit to memory, and recite and rehearse in my own room, over and over again; yet when the day came, when the school collected to hear declamations, when my name was called, and I saw all eyes turned to my seat, I could not raise myself from it. When the occasion was over I went home and wept bitter tears of mortification."

After leaving Dartmouth he studied law and in 1805 was admitted to the bar. He rapidly became prominent in his profession and finally settled at Boston. He was elected to Congress and for thirty-four years was in public life as representative, as senator, and twice as Secretary of State.

His two speeches at the Bunker Hill Monument, his eulogy on Jefferson and Adams, and his speech in the White murder trial, together with his Reply to Hayne, are his greatest efforts and are worthy their reputation among the finest examples of classic eloquence.

Some knowledge of the circumstances under which his *Reply to Hayne* was given is necessary to an appreciation of it.

On the twenty-ninth of December, 1829, Mr. Foote of Connecticut introduced the apparently harmless resolution which precipitated the great debate. It was a simple inquiry into the quantity of public lands unsold and into the expediency of abolishing some of the land offices and of limiting or hastening the sales of such lands. The southern members claimed to see in this resolution some menace to their rights and the opportunity was seized to make a bitter personal attack upon New England men, and Mr. Webster in particular.

Webster had nothing to do with the introduction of the resolution and did not know it would be made the occasion for such a debate. It is claimed by some that the whole attack was part of a formal conspiracy to overthrow Webster's power and influence and array the new west against New England and its leaders, while the south was to be considered the sympathetic ally of the west.

The debate continued with occasional interruptions for four months and engaged the greatest men of both parties. Benton and Hayne were most conspicuous in vituperative brilliancy and vehement offensiveness. Others sided with them. President Jackson was openly and consistently opposed to Webster, and Vice-President John C. Calhoun, the presiding officer of the Senate, was an avowed leader, and a frequent aid to Hayne in his last brilliant speech.

It was on Monday, the 18th of January, that Benton and Hayne made their first violent attack upon New England. Though their bitterness and virulency surprised Mr. Webster he arose to reply but yielded to an adjournment as it was then a late hour. The next day he replied but his speech was not conclusive.

On Thursday the debate was resumed by Mr. Hayne. Webster was engaged in an important case before the Supreme Court and his attendance there seemed necessary, but though a friend asked an adjournment, to enable Webster to be present, Hayne would not consent. He said he had something here (placing his hand on his heart) that he wished to get rid of. Webster had discharged his fire in the face of the Speaker and Hayne demanded an opportunity to return the shot. An eye witness says: "Then it was that Mr. Webster's person seemed to become taller and bigger. His chest expanded and his eyeballs dilated. Folding his arms in a composed, firm and most expressive manner, he exclaimed: 'Let the discussion proceed. I am ready. I am ready *now* to receive the gentleman's fire.'"

In the speech that followed, Hayne confident of success used every art of the skillful debater and showed himself a master of stinging eloquence. What he said, at least many of the most caustic remarks, may be inferred from Webster's reply but the effect of his words can only be imagined. His friends crowded around him and were as confident of victory as their arrogant leader.

This was on Thursday. An adjournment followed and it was the Tuesday following, January 26, 1830, that Webster again appeared upon the floor. In the meantime he had thought much, and hesitated greatly whether it were best to advance freely his views on the constitution, views which came as the result of years of close study and deep meditation. But his friends urged him to withhold nothing, to crush at one blow the doctrine of a state's right to nullify a law of the

government, for to this point had the debate now
swung. Accordingly when the hour arrived, the
great orator was fully prepared to defend himself
and his New England friends and then to unfold
this most masterly exposition of the relation of
the constitution to the states.

At the capital, interest was never greater.
Other public business was at a standstill; the
House of Representatives was deserted, its members crowding into the Senate which was full to
its utmost, long before the speech began. The
galleries, the floor, the aisles, and the space about
the President's desk, were all filled with expectant
men. Such an audience has rarely met a speaker
and not often has an orator held an audience in
such spell-bound attention. Master of his subject and master of his hearers, Webster began.
He was in the very perfection of his manhood,
strong, imposing, self-reliant. His tremendous
personal vigor and his dignified poise, his stal-
wart frame and massive head, his fiery eyes glanc-
ing beneath their overhanging brows, and his deep
and resonant voice, all united to lend force and
conviction to his ponderous rhetoric.

Though much of his speech is argumentation,
plain and unadorned, yet those who listened never
abated their thrilling interest till the orator had
ceased. One who was present says: "The
speech was over, but the tones of the orator still
lingered upon the ear, and the audience, uncon-

scious of its close, retained their position. The agitated countenance, the heaving breast, the suffused eye, attested the continued influence of the spell upon them. Hands that in the excitement of the moment had sought each other, still remained closed in unconscious grasp. Eye still turned to eye, to receive and repay mutual sympathy, and everywhere around seemed forgetfulness of all but the orator's presence and words."

Reply to Hayne

DANIEL WEBSTER

Reply to Hayne

In the U. S. Senate, January 26, 1830.

MR. PRESIDENT,— When the mariner has been tossed for many days in thick weather and on an unknown sea, he naturally avails himself of the first pause in the storm, the earliest glance of the sun, to take his latitude and ascertain how far the elements have driven him from his true course. Let us imitate this prudence, and, before we float farther on the waves of this debate, refer to the point from which we departed, that we may at least be able to conjecture where we now are. I ask for the reading of the resolution.

The secretary read the resolution, as follows :

"*Resolved*, That the committee on public lands be instructed to inquire and report the quantity of public lands remaining unsold within each State and Territory, and whether it be expedient to limit for a certain period the sales of the public lands to such lands only as

NOTE.—Owing to the great length of this speech some portions have been omitted, but enough of comment is made in their places to preserve the meaning of the context.

43

have heretofore been offered for sale, and are now subject to entry at the minimum price. And, also, whether the office of surveyor-general, and some of the land offices, may not be abolished without detriment to the public interest; or whether it be expedient to adopt measures to hasten the sales and extend more rapidly the surveys of the public lands."

We have thus heard, sir, what the resolution is which is actually before us for consideration; and it will readily occur to every one that it is almost the only subject about which something has not been said in the speech, running through two days, by which the senate has been now entertained by the gentleman from South Carolina. Every topic in the wide range of our public affairs, whether past or present — everything, general or local, whether belonging to national politics or party politics — seems to have attracted more or less of the honorable member's attention, save only the resolution before the senate. He has spoken of everything but the public lands; they have escaped his notice. To that subject, in all his excursions, he has not paid even the cold respect of a passing glance.

When this debate, sir, was to be resumed, on Thursday morning, it so happened that it would have been convenient for me to be elsewhere.[1] The honorable member, however, did not incline to put off the discussion to another day. He had a shot, he said, to return, and he wished to discharge it. That shot, sir, which it was kind thus to inform us was coming, that we might stand out of the way, or prepare ourselves to fall before it and die with decency, has now been received. Under all advantages, and with expectation awakened by the tone which preceded it, it has been discharged, and has spent its force. It may become me to say no more of its effect, than that, if nobody is found, after all, either killed or wounded by it, it is not the first time, in the history of human affairs, that the vigor and success of the war have not quite come up to the lofty and sounding phrase of the manifesto.

The gentleman, sir, in declining to postpone the debate, told the senate, with the emphasis of his hand upon his heart, that there was something rankling *here*, which he wished to relieve.

---

1. Mr. Webster was one of the attorneys in an important case known as *Carriers' Lessees* against *John Jacob Astor*, then on trial before the supreme court.

[Mr. Hayne rose and disclaimed the use of the word *rankling.*]

It would not, sir, be safe for the honorable member to appeal to those around him, upon the question whether he did in fact make use of that word. But he may have been unconscious of it. At any rate, it is enough that he disclaims it. But still, with or without the use of that particular word, he had yet something *here*, he said, of which he wished to rid himself by an immediate reply. In this respect, sir, I have a great advantage over the honorable gentleman. There is nothing *here*, sir, which gives me the slightest uneasiness; neither fear, nor anger, nor that which is sometimes more troublesome than either, the consciousness of having been in the wrong. There is nothing either originating *here*, or now received *here*, by the gentleman's shot. Nothing originating here, for I had not the slightest feeling of disrespect or unkindness toward the honorable member. Some passages,[2] it is true, had occurred since our acquaintance in this body, which I could have wished might have been

---

2. The Panama Congress was called by the Republic of South America in 1826. President Adams, Webster and some others were strongly in favor of the meeting, and delegates were sent by the United States. Webster called on the President for instructions to these ministers. Hayne vigorously opposed the entire movement.

otherwise; but I had used philosophy and forgotten them. When the honorable member
rose in his first speech, I paid him the respect
of attentive listening; and when he sat down,
though surprised, and I must say even aston-
ished, at some of his opinions, nothing was
farther from my intention than to commence
any personal warfare. And through the whole
of the few remarks I made in answer, I
avoided, studiously and carefully, everything
which I thought possible to be construed into
disrespect. And, sir, while there is thus
nothing originating *here* which I wished at
any time, or now wish, to discharge, I must
repeat also, that nothing has been received
here which *rankles*, or in any way gives me
annoyance. I will not accuse the honorable
member of violating the rules of civilized war;
I will not say that he poisoned his arrows.
But whether his shafts were, or were not,
dipped in that which would have caused rankling if they had reached, there was not, as it
happened, quite strength enough in the bow
to bring them to their mark. If he wishes
now to gather up those shafts he must look
for them elsewhere; they will not be found
fixed and quivering in the object at which
they were aimed.

The honorable member complained that I had slept on his speech. I must have slept on it, or not slept at all. The moment the honorable member sat down, his friend from Missouri[3] rose, and, with much honeyed commendation of the speech, suggested that the impressions which it had produced were too charming and delightful to be disturbed by other sentiments or other sounds, and proposed that the senate should adjourn. Would it have been quite amiable in me, sir, to interrupt this excellent good feeling? Must I not have been absolutely malicious, if I could have thrust myself forward, to destroy sensations thus pleasing? Was it not much better and kinder, both to sleep upon them myself, and to allow others also the pleasure of sleeping upon them? But if it be meant, by sleeping upon his speech, that I took time to prepare a reply to it, it is quite a mistake. Owing to other engagements, I could not employ even the interval between the adjournment of the senate and its meeting the next morning, in attention to the subject of this debate. Nevertheless, sir, the mere matter of fact is undoubtedly true. I did sleep on the gentle-

---

3. Hon. Thomas H. Benton.

man's speech, and slept soundly. And I slept equally well on his speech of yesterday, to which I am now replying. It is quite possible that in this respect, also, I possess some advantage over the honorable member, attributable, doubtless, to a cooler temperament on my part; for, in truth, I slept upon his speeches remarkably well.

But the gentleman inquires why *he* was made the object of such a reply. Why was he singled out? If an attack has been made on the east, he, he assures us, did not begin it; it was made by the gentleman from Missouri. Sir, I answered the gentleman's speech because I happened to hear it; and because, also, I chose to give an answer to that speech, which, if unanswered, I thought most likely to produce injurious impressions. I did not stop to inquire who was the original drawer of the bill. I found a responsible indorser before me, and it was my purpose to hold him liable, and to bring him to his just responsibility without delay. But, sir, this interrogatory of the honorable member was only introductory to another. He proceeded to ask me whether I had turned upon him, in this debate, from the consciousness that I should find an overmatch, if I ventured on a contest with his friend from Missouri.[4] If, sir, the honorable member, *ex gratia modestiæ*,[5] had chosen thus to defer to his friend, and to pay him a compliment, without intentional disparagement to others, it would have been quite according to the friendly courtesies of debate, and not at all ungrateful to my own feelings. I am not one of those, sir, who esteem any tribute of regard, whether light and occasional, or more serious and deliberate, which may be bestowed on others, as so much unjustly withholden from themselves. But the tone and manner of the gentleman's question forbid me thus to interpret it. I am not at liberty to consider it as nothing more than a civility to his friend. It had an air of taunt and disparagement, something of the loftiness of asserted superiority, which does not allow me to pass it over without notice. It was put as a question for me to answer, and so put as if it were difficult for me to answer, whether I deemed the member from Missouri an overmatch for myself in

4. During the course of the debate upon Foote's resolutions, Mr. Hayne and Mr. Benton had condemned the policy of the eastern states as being illiberal to the west. Mr. Webster replied in vindication of New England and the policy of the government.

5. From modest grace.

debate here. It seems to me, sir, that this is extraordinary language, and an extraordinary tone for the discussions of this body.

Matches and overmatches! Those terms are more applicable elsewhere than here, and fitter for other assemblies than this. Sir, the gentleman seems to forget where and what we are. This is a senate, a senate of equals, of men of individual honor and personal character, and of absolute independence. We know no masters, we acknowledge no dictators. This is a hall for mutual consultation and discussion; not an arena for the exhibition of champions. I offer myself, sir, as a match for no man ; I throw the challenge of debate at no man's feet. But then, sir, since the honorable member has put the question in a manner that calls for an answer, I will give him an answer ; and I tell him, that, holding myself to be the humblest of the members here, I yet know nothing in the arm of his friend from Missouri, either alone or when aided by the arm of *his* friend from South Carolina, that need deter even me from espousing whatever opinions I may choose to espouse, from debating whenever I may choose to debate, or from speaking whatever I may see fit to say, on the floor of the senate.

But, sir, the coalition ! [6]   The coalition !
Ay, "the murdered coalition !"   The gentleman asks, if I were led or frighted into this
debate by the specter of the coalition.   "Was
it the ghost of the murdered coalition," he
exclaims, "which haunted the member from
Massachusetts, and which, like the ghost of
Banquo, [7] would never down?"   "The murdered coalition !"   Sir, this charge of a coalition, in reference to the late administration,
is not original with the honorable member.
It did not spring up in the senate.   Whether
as a fact, as an argument, or as an embel-
lishment, it is all borrowed.   He adopts it,
indeed, from a very low origin, and a still
lower present condition.   It is one of the
thousand calumnies with which the press
teemed during an excited political canvass.
It was a charge, of which there was not
only no proof or probability, but which was

---

6. The coalition. There were four candidates at the presidential
election in 1824. As no candidate received a majority of the electoral
votes, the election went to the House of Representatives. The friends
of John Quincy Adams and Henry Clay united and elected Adams. The
Jacksonian party accused Clay of forming a coalition with Adams, and
selling out to him, on condition that Clay should be made secretary of
state. Clay was appointed to this position, and the belief that such a
bargain had been made was quite current for some years. A complete understanding of the situation later, however, entirely disproved the charge.

7. Banquo, murdered by Macbeth. The allusion is to the ghost that
appeared at the banquet in Shakespeare's play. See Part Twelve.

in itself wholly impossible to be true. No man of common information ever believed a syllable of it. Yet it was of that class of falsehoods which, by continued repetition, through all the organs of detraction and abuse, are capable of misleading those who are already far misled, and of further fanning passion already kindling into flame. Doubtless it served in its day, and in greater or less degree the end designed by it. Having done that, it has sunk into the general mass of stale and loathed calumnies. It is the very cast-off slough of a polluted and shameless press. Incapable of further mischief, it lies in the sewer, lifeless and despised. It is not now, sir, in the power of the honorable member to give it dignity and decency, by attempting to elevate it, and to introduce it into the senate. He can not change it from what it is, an object of general disgust and scorn. On the contrary, the contact, if he choose to touch it, is more likely to drag him down, down, to the place where it lies itself.

But, sir, the honorable member was not, for other reasons, entirely happy in his allusion to the story of Banquo's murder and Banquo's ghost. It was not, I think, the friends, but the enemies of the murdered

Banquo, at whose bidding his spirit would not *down*. The honorable gentleman is fresh in his reading of the English classics, and can put me right if I am wrong; but, according to my poor recollection, it was at those who had begun with caresses and ended with foul and treacherous murder that the gory locks were shaken. The ghost of Banquo, like that of Hamlet,[8] was an honest ghost. It disturbed no innocent man. It knew where its appearance would strike terror, and who would cry out, A ghost! It made itself visible in the right quarter, and compelled the guilty and the conscience-smitten, and none others, to start, with,

"Prythee, see there! behold! — look; lo!
If I stand here, I saw him!"

Their eyeballs were seared (was it not so, sir?) who had thought to shield themselves by concealing their own hand, and laying the imputation of the crime on a low and hireling agency in wickedness; who had vainly attempted to stifle the workings of their own coward consciences by ejaculating through

8. The ghost of the king, Hamlet's father, that came to tell his son how he had been murdered.

white lips and chattering teeth, "Thou canst not say I did it!" I have misread the great poet if those who had no way partaken in the deed of the death either found that they were, or *feared that they should be*, pushed from their stools by the ghost of the slain, or exclaimed to a specter created by their own fears and their own remorse, "Avaunt! and quit our sight!"

There is another particular, sir, in which the honorable member's quick perception of resemblances might, I should think, have seen something in the story of Banquo making it not altogether a subject of the most pleasant contemplation. Those who murdered Banquo, what did they win by it? Substantial good? Permanent power? Or disappointment, rather, and sore mortification; dust and ashes the common fate of vaulting ambition overleaping itself? Did not even-handed justice ere long commend the poisoned chalice to their own lips? Did they not soon find that for another they had "'filed their mind?" that their ambition, though apparently for the moment successful, had but put a barren scepter in their grasp? Ay, sir, "a barren scepter in their gripe

*Thence to be wrenched by an unlineal hand,
No son of theirs succeeding."* [9]

Sir, I need pursue the allusion no farther. I leave the honorable gentleman to run it out at his leisure, and to derive from it all the gratification it is calculated to administer. If he finds himself pleased with the associations, and prepared to be quite satisfied, though the parallel should be entirely completed, I had almost said, I am satisfied also; but that I shall think of. Yes, sir, I will think of that. . . .

I spoke, sir, of the Ordinance of 1787, which prohibited slavery, in all future times, northwest of the Ohio, as a measure of great wisdom and foresight, and one which had been attended with highly beneficial and permanent consequences. I supposed that, on this point, no two gentlemen in the senate could entertain different opinions. But the simple expression of this sentiment has led the gentleman, not only into a labored defense of

---

9. This is a sarcastic reference to Calhoun's future prospects. Calhoun was anxious to secure the next election to the presidency, but his relations to President Jackson were such that it was evident that Van Buren would be the choice of the party.

slavery, in the abstract and on principle, but also into a warm accusation against me, as having attacked the system of domestic slavery now existing in the southern states. For all this there was not the slightest foundation in anything said or intimated by me. I did not utter a single word which any ingenuity could torture into an attack on the slavery of the south. I said, only, that it was highly wise and useful, in legislating for the north-western country while it was yet a wilderness, to prohibit the introduction of slaves; and added, that I presumed there was in the neighboring state of Kentucky no reflecting and intelligent gentleman who would doubt that, if the same prohibition had been extended at the same early period, over that commonwealth, her strength and population would, at this day, have been far greater than they are. If these opinions be thought doubtful, they are nevertheless, I trust, neither extraordinary nor disrespectful. They attack nobody and menace nobody. And yet, sir, the gentleman's optics have discovered, even in the mere expresssion of this sentiment, what he calls the very spirit of the Missouri question. He represents me as making an onset on the whole south, and manifesting a spirit

57

which would interfere with and disturb their domestic condition !

Sir, this injustice no otherwise surprises me, than as it is committed here, and committed without the slightest pretense of ground for it. I say it only surprises me as being done here; for I know full well, that it is and has been, the settled policy of some persons in the south, for years, to represent the people of the north as disposed to interfere with them in their own exclusive and peculiar concerns. This is a delicate and sensitive point in southern feeling; and of late years it has always been touched, and generally with effect, whenever the object has been to unite the whole south against northern men or northern measures. This feeling, always carefully kept alive, and maintained at too intense a heat to admit discrimination or reflection, is a lever of great power in our political machine. It moves vast bodies, and gives to them one and the same direction. But it is without any adequate cause, and the suspicion which exists is wholly groundless. There is not, and never has been, a disposition in the north to interfere with these interests of the south. Such interference has never been supposed to be within the power of government; nor has it been in any way attempted. The slavery of the south has always been regarded as a matter of domestic policy, left with the states themselves, and with which the federal government had nothing to do. Certainly, sir, I am, and ever have been, of that opinion. The gentleman, indeed, argues that slavery, in the abstract, is no evil. Most assuredly I need not say I differ with him, altogether and most widely, on that point. I regard domestic slavery as one of the greatest of evils, both moral and political. But though it be a malady, and whether it be curable, and if so, by what means; or, on the other hand, whether it be the *vulnus immedicabile* [10] of the social system, I leave it to those whose right and duty it is to inquire and to decide. And this I believe, sir, is, and uniformly has been, the sentiment of the north.

(Several pages are here omitted. In them, Webster looks a little into history. He reviews the relation of slavery to the constitution and shows that congress had passed resolutions denying the right of that body to interfere in the treatment of slaves in any of the states, and this by a congress composed largely of northern men. He

10. Incurable wound.

recognizes the advantages of representation to be with the south, but does not complain. He favors the constitution as it is and the Union as it is, but he resents the imputation that he is seeking to extend the power of the government over the internal laws of the states. He discusses the Ordinance of 1787, and shows that it was due to the influence and votes of northern men that slavery was prohibited in the Northwest Territory, and that free schools were secured there.)

But as to the Hartford convention,[11] sir, allow me to say, that the proceedings of that body seem now to be less read and studied in New England than farther south. They appear to be looked to, not in New England, but elsewhere, for the purpose of seeing how far they may serve as a precedent. But they will not answer the purpose, they are quite too tame. The latitude in which they originated was too cold. Other conventions, of more recent existence, have gone a whole bar's length beyond it. The learned doctors of Colleton

---

11. The Hartford convention met at Hartford, Conn., Dec. 15, 1814. It was composed of delegates from Massachusetts, Connecticut, and Rhode Island, and was the outgrowth of the opposition of the Federalists to the war. Its sessions were behind closed doors, and a report was falsely circulated that it proposed measures leading to the secession of the New England states from the Union. The proceedings brought discredit upon the Federalists of New England.

and Abbeville [12] have pushed their commentaries on the Hartford collect so far, that the original text-writers are thrown entirely into the shade. I have nothing to do, sir, with the Hartford convention. Its journal, which the gentleman has quoted, I never read. So far as the honorable member may discover in its proceedings a spirit in any degree resembling that which was avowed and justified in those other conventions to which I have alluded, or so far as those proceedings can be shown to be disloyal to the constitution, or tending to disunion, so far I shall be as ready as any one to bestow. on them reprehension and censure.

Having dwelt long on this convention, and other occurrences of that day, in the hope, probably, (which will not be gratified,) that I should leave the course of this debate to follow him at length in those excursions, the honorable member returned, and attempted another object. He referred to a speech of mine in the other house, the same which I had 'occasion to allude to myself, the other day; and has quoted a passage or two from it,

---

12. Hayne was born in the Colleton district, and Calhoun in the Abbeville district of South Carolina. Anti-tariff meetings had been held in bot'ι districts in 1828, and the reference is probably to them.

with a bold, though uneasy and laboring air of confidence, as if he had detected in me an inconsistency. Judging from the gentleman's manner, a stranger to the course of the debate and to the point in discussion would have imagined, from so triumphant a tone, that the honorable member was about to overwhelm me with a manifest contradiction. Any one who heard him, and who had not heard what I had, in fact, previously said, must have thought me routed and discomfited, as the gentleman had promised. Sir, a breath blows all this triumph away. There is not the slightest difference in the sentiments of my remarks on the two occasions. What I said here on Wednesday is in exact accordance with the opinion expressed by me in the other house in 1825. Though the gentleman had the metaphysics of Hudibras,[13] though he were able

"to sever and divide
A hair 'twixt north and northwest side,"

he yet could not insert his metaphysical scissors between the fair reading of my remarks in 1825 and what I said here last week. There

---

13. In Butler's satire a Presbyterian justice of the peace who sets out to reform abuses, to suppress games and amusements.

is not only no contradiction, no difference, but, in truth, too exact a similarity, both in thought and language, to be entirely in just taste. I had myself quoted the same speech; had recurred to it, and spoke with it open before me; and much of what I said was little more than a repetition from it.

*　　*　　*　　*　　*

I need not repeat at large the general topics of the honorable gentleman's speech. When he said yesterday that he did not attack the eastern states, he certainly must have forgotten, not only particular remarks, but the whole drift and tenor of his speech; unless he means by not attacking, that he did not commence hostilities, but that another had preceded him in the attack. He, in the first place, disapproved of the whole course of the government, for forty years, in regard to its disposition of the public land; and then, turning northward and eastward, and fancying he had found a cause for alleged narrowness and niggardliness in the "accursed policy" of the tariff, to which he represented the people of New England as wedded, he went on for a full hour with remarks, the whole scope of which was to exhibit the results of this policy, in feelings and in measures unfavorable to the west. I thought his opinions unfounded and erroneous as to the general course of the government, and ventured to reply to them.

The gentleman had remarked on the analogy of other cases, and quoted the conduct of European governments toward their own subjects settling on this continent as in point, to show that we had been harsh and rigid in selling, when we should have given the public lands to settlers without price. I thought the honorable member had suffered his judgment to be betrayed by a false analogy; that he was struck with an appearance of resemblance where there was no real similitude. I think so still. The first settlers of North America were enterprising spirits, engaged in private adventure, or fleeing from tyranny at home. When arrived here, they were forgotten by the mother country, or remembered only to be oppressed. Carried away again by the appearance of analogy, or struck with the eloquence of the passage, the honorable member yesterday observed that the conduct of government toward the western emigrants, or my representation of it, brought to his mind a celebrated speech in the British parliament. It was, sir, the speech of Colonel Barre. On the question of the stamp act, or tea tax, I forget which, Colonel Barre had heard a member on the treasury bench argue, that the people of the United States, being British colonists, planted by the maternal care, nourished by the indulgence, and protected by the arms of England, would not grudge their mite to relieve the mother country from the heavy burden under which she groaned. The language of Colonel Barre, in reply to this, was: ''They planted by your care? Your oppression planted them in America. They fled from your tyranny, and grew by your neglect of them. So soon as you began to care for them, you showed your care by sending persons to spy out their liberties, misrepresent their character, prey upon them, and eat out their substance.''

And how does the honorable gentleman mean to maintain that language like this is applicable to the conduct of the government of the United States toward the western emigrants, or to any representation given by me of that conduct? Were the settlers in the west driven thither by our oppression? Have they flourished only by our neglect of them? Has the government done nothing but to prey upon them, and eat out their substance? Sir, this fervid eloquence of the British speaker, just when and where it was uttered, and fit to remain an exercise for the schools, is not a little out of place when it is brought thence to be applied here, to the conduct of our own country toward her own citizens. From America to England, it may be true; from Americans to their own government, it would be strange language. Let us leave it to be recited and declaimed by our boys against a foreign nation; not introduce it here, to recite and declaim ourselves against our own.

(Webster reiterates his views as to the proper method of handling the public lands and brings his opponent back to the real question. Has the doctrine been advanced at the south or the east that the population of the west should be retarded or at least not be hastened? Is this doctrine of eastern origin? New England is guiltless of any such policy.)

We approach, at length, sir, to a more important part of the honorable gentleman's observation. Since it does not accord with my views of justice and policy to give away the public lands altogether, as mere matter of gratuity, I am asked by the honorable gentleman on what ground it is that I consent to vote them away in particular instances.

How, he inquires, do I reconcile with these professed sentiments my support of measures appropriating portions of the lands to particular roads, particular canals, particular rivers, and particular institutions of education in the west? This leads, sir, to the real and wide difference in political opinion between the honorable gentleman and myself. On my part, I look upon all these objects as connected with the common good, fairly embraced in its object and its terms; he, on the contrary, deems them all, if good at all, only local good. This is our difference. The interrogatory which he proceeded to put, at once explains this difference. "What interest," asks he, "has South Carolina in a canal in Ohio?" Sir, this very question is full of significance. It develops the gentleman's whole political system; and its answer expounds mine. Here we differ. I look upon a road over the Alleghanies, a canal round the falls of the Ohio, or a canal or railway from the Atlantic to the western waters, as being an object large and extensive enough to be fairly said to be for the common benefit.[14]

14. The question of internal improvements at public expense was one upon which the older political parties divided. Since 1789, money has been steadily appropriated by congress for the building of lighthouses, and other coast improvements, but the first actual appropriation for a

The gentleman thinks otherwise, and this is the key to his construction of the powers of the government. He may well ask what interest has South Carolina in a canal in Ohio. On his system, it is true, she has no interest. On that system, Ohio and Carolina are different governments and different countries; connected here, it is true, by some slight and ill-defined bond of union, but in all main respects separate and diverse. On that system Carolina has no more interest in a canal in Ohio than in Mexico. The gentleman, therefore, only follows out his own principles; he does no more than arrive at the natural conclusions of his own doctrines; he only announces the true results of that creed which he has adopted himself, and would persuade others to adopt, when he thus declares that South Carolina has no interest in a public work in Ohio.

Sir, we narrow-minded people of New England do not reason thus. Our *notion* of things is entirely different. We look upon the states, not as separated, but as united. We love to dwell on that union, and on the

---

strictly internal improvement was in 1806, when money was granted for the construction of the Cumberland Road from Cumberland on the Potomac to the Ohio. This road was continued as far as Illinois in 1838. John Quincy Adams and his followers advocated such measures and the fact was instrumental in his defeat for a second term. At the time of the great debate the discussion of this policy was becoming somewhat bitter.

ROBERT YOUNG HAYNE

mutual happiness which it has so much pro-
moted, and the common renown which it has
so greatly contributed to acquire.   In our contemplation, Carolina and Ohio are parts of the
same country; states united under the same
general government, having interests common, associated, intermingled.   In whatever
is within the proper sphere of the constitutional power of this government, we look
upon the states as one.   We do not impose
geographical limits to our patriotic feeling or
regard; we do not follow rivers and mountains,
and lines of latitude, to find boundaries beyond which public improvements do not benefit
us.   We who come here as agents and representatives of these narrow-minded and selfish
men of New England, consider ourselves as
bound to regard with an equal eye the good of
the whole, in whatever is within our power of
legislation.   Sir, if a railroad or canal, beginning in South Carolina and ending in South
Carolina, appeared to me to be of national
importance and national magnitude, believing,
as I do, that the power of government extends
to the encouragement of works of that description, if I were to stand up here and ask,
What interest has Massachusetts in a railroad
in South Carolina?   I should not be willing to

face my constituents. These same narrow-minded men would tell me, that they had sent me to act for the whole country, and that one who possessed too little comprehension, either of intellect or feeling, one who was not large enough, both in mind and in heart, to embrace the whole, was not fit to be intrusted with the interest of any part.

Sir, I do not desire to enlarge the powers of the government by unjustifiable construction, nor to exercise any not within a fair interpretation. But when it is believed that a power does exist, then it is, in my judgment, to be exercised for the general benefit of the whole. So far as respects the exercise of such a power, the states are one. It was the very object of the constitution to create unity of interests to the extent of the powers of the general government. In war and peace we are one; in commerce, one; because the authority of the general government reaches to war and peace, and to the regulation of commerce. I have never seen any more difficulty in erecting lighthouses on the lakes, than on the ocean; in improving the harbors of inland seas, than if they were within the ebb and flow of the tide; or in removing obstructions in the vast streams of the west, more then in any work to facilitate commerce on the Atlantic coast. If there be any power for one, there is power also for the other ; and they are all and equally for the common good of the country.

(The proceeds of the public lands should be a common fund for the benefit of the new states. This principle northern votes have established. Hayne has asked *when, how,* and *why* New England votes were found going for measures favorable to the west, and insinuates that it began in 1825 and while a presidential election was pending.)

Sir, to these questions retort would be justified; and it is both cogent and at hand. Nevertheless, I will answer the inquiry, not by retort, but by facts. I will tell the gentleman *when,* and *how,* and *why* New England has supported measures favorable to the west. I have already referred to the early history of the government, to the first acquisition of the lands, to the original laws for disposing of them, and for governing the territories where they lie; and have shown the influence of New England men and New England principles in all these leading measures. I should not be pardoned were I to go over that ground again. Coming to more recent times, and to

measures of a less general character, I have
endeavored to prove that everything of this
kind, designed for western improvement, has
depended on the votes of New England ; all
this is true beyond the power of contradiction. And now, sir, there are two measures
to which I will refer, not so ancient as to belong to the early history of the public lands,
and not so recent as to be on this side of the
period when the gentleman charitably imag-
ines a new direction may have been given to
New England feeling and New England votes.
These measures, and the New England votes
in support of them, may be taken as samples
and specimens of all the rest.

In 1820 (observe, Mr. President, in 1820),
the people of the west besought congress for
a reduction in the price of lands. In favor of
that reduction, New England, with a delega-
tion of forty members in the other house, gave
thirty-three votes, and one only against it.
The four southern states, with over fifty members, gave thirty-two votes for it, and seven
against it. Again, in 1821 (observe again, sir,
the time), the law passed for the relief of the
purchasers of the public lands. This was a
measure of vital importance to the west, and
more especially to the southwest. It author-

ized the relinquishment of contracts for lands which had been entered into at high prices, and a reduction in other cases of not less than thirty-seven and a half per cent on the purchase-money. Many millions of dollars, six or seven I believe, at least — probably much more — were relinquished by this law. On this bill, New England, with her forty members, gave more affirmative votes than the four southern states, with their fifty-two or three members. These two are far the most important general measures respecting the public lands which have been adopted within the last twenty years. They took place in 1820 and 1821. That is the time *when*.

As to the manner *how*, the gentleman already sees that it was by voting in solid column for the required relief. And, lastly, as to the cause *why*, I tell the gentleman it was because the members from New England thought the measures just and salutary; because they entertained toward the west neither envy, hatred, nor malice ; because they deemed it becoming them, as just and enlightened men, to meet the exigency which had arisen in the west with the appropriate measure of relief; because they felt it due to their own characters, and the characters of their New England predecessors in this government, to act toward the new states in the spirit of a liberal, patronizing, magnanimous policy. So much, sir, for the cause *why*, and I hope that by this time, sir, the honorable gentleman is satisfied; if not, I do not know *when*, or *how*, or *why* he ever will be. . . .

This government, Mr. President, from its origin to the peace of 1815, had been too much engrossed with various other important concerns to be able to turn its thoughts inward, and look to the development of its vast internal resources. In the early part of President Washington's administration, it was fully occupied with completing its own organization, providing for the public debt, defending the frontiers, and maintaining domestic peace. Before the termination of that administration, the fires of the French revolution blazed forth, as from a new-opened volcano, and the whole breadth of the ocean did not secure us from its effects. The smoke and the cinders reached us, though not the burning lava. Difficult and agitating questions, embarrassing to government and dividing public opinion, sprung out of the new state of our foreign relations, and were succeeded by others, and yet again by others, equally embarrassing and equally exciting division and discord, through the long series of twenty years, till they finally issued in the war with England. Down to the close of that war, no distinct, marked, and deliberate attention had been given, or could have been given, to the internal condition of the country, its capacities of improvement, or the constitutional power of the government in regard to objects connected with such improvement.

The peace, Mr. President, brought about an entirely new and a most interesting state of things ; it opened to us other prospects and suggested other duties. We ourselves were changed, and the whole world was changed. The pacification of Europe, after June, 1815, assumed a firm and permanent aspect. The nations evidently manifested that they were disposed for peace. Some agitation of the waves might be expected, even after the storm had subsided, but the tendency was, strongly and rapidly, toward settled repose.

It so happened, sir, that I was at that time a member of congress, and, like others, naturally turned my attention to the contemplation of the newly altered condition of the country and of the world. It appeared plainly enough to me, as well as to wiser and more experienced men, that the policy of the government would naturally take a start in a new direction; because new directions would necessarily be given to the pursuits and occupations of the people. We had pushed our commerce far and fast, under the advantage of a neutral flag. But there were now no longer flags, either neutral or belligerent. The harvest of neutrality had been great, but we had gathered it all. With the peace of Europe, it was obvious there would spring up in her circle of nations a revived and invigorating spirit of trade, and a new activity in all the business and objects of civilized life. Hereafter, our commercial gains were to be earned only by success in a close and intense competition. Other nations would produce for themselves, and carry for themselves, and manufacture for themselves, to the full extent of their abilities. The crops of our plains would no longer sustain European armies, nor our ships longer supply those whom war had rendered unable to supply themselves. It was obvious that, under these circumstances, the country would begin to survey itself, and to estimate its own capacity of improvement.

And this improvement — how was it to be

accomplished, and who was to accomplish
it? We were ten or twelve millions of
people, spread over almost half a world.
We were more than twenty states, some
stretching along the same seaboard, some
along the same line of inland frontier, and
others on opposite banks of the same vast
rivers. Two considerations at once presented
themselves, in looking at this state of things,
with great force. One was, that that great
branch of improvement which consisted in
furnishing new facilities of intercourse necessarily ran into different states in every leading
instance, and would benefit the citizens of all
such states. No one state, therefore, in such
cases, would assume the whole expense, nor
was the coöperation of several states to be expected. Take the instance of the Delaware
breakwater.[5] It will cost several millions of
money. Would Pennsylvania alone ever have
constructed it? Certainly never, while this
Union lasts, because it is not for her sole
benefit. Would Pennsylvania, New Jersey,
and Delaware have united to accomplish it at
their joint expense? Certainly not, for the

---

15. The Delaware breakwater was authorized by congress in 1829, and
work was begun at Cape Henlopen. In 1869 the work was completed, and
Delaware Bay was made an excellent harbor.

same reason. It could not be done, therefore, but by the general government. The same may be said of the large inland undertakings, except that, in them, government, instead of bearing the whole expense, coöperates with others who bear a part. The other consideration is, that the United States have the means. They enjoy the revenues derived from commerce, and the states have no abundant and easy sources of public income. The custom-houses fill the general treasury, while the states have scanty resources, except by resort to heavy direct taxes.

Under this view of things, I thought it necessary to settle, at least for myself, some definite notions with respect to the powers of the government with regard to internal affairs. It may not savor too much of self-commendation to remark, that, with this object, I considered the constitution, its judicial construction, its contemporaneous exposition, and the whole history of the legislation of congress under it; and I arrived at the conclusion, that government had power to accomplish sundry objects, or aid in their accomplishment, which are now commonly spoken of as INTERNAL IMPROVEMENTS.

That conclusion, sir, may have been right, or it may have been wrong. I am not about to argue the grounds of it at large. I say only, that it was adopted and acted on even so early as in 1816. Yes, Mr. President, I made up my 'opinion, and determined on my intended course of political conduct, on these subjects, in the fourteenth congress, in 1816. And now, Mr. President, I have further to say, that I made up these opinions, and entered on this course of political conduct, *Teucro duce*. [16] Yes, sir, I pursued in all this a South Carolina track. On the doctrines of internal improvement, South Carolina, as she was then represented in the other house, set forth in 1816 under a fresh and leading breeze, and I was among the followers. But if my leader sees new lights and turns a sharp corner, unless I see new lights also, I keep straight on in the same path. I repeat, that leading gentlemen from South Carolina were first and foremost in behalf of the doctrines of internal improvements, when those doctrines came first to be considered and acted upon in congress. The debate on the bank question,

---

16. *Teucer being the leader.* Teucer was one of the leaders of the Greeks in the Trojan war. Mr. Calhoun was then President of the Senate, being Vice-President of the United States.

on the tariff of 1816, and on the direct tax, will show who was who, and what was what, at that time.

The tariff of 1816 (one of the plain cases of oppression and usurpation, from which, if the government does not recede, individual states may justly secede from the government) is, sir, in truth, a South Carolina tariff, supported by South Carolina votes. But for those votes it could not have passed in the form in which it did pass; whereas, if it had depended on Massachusetts votes, it would have been lost. Does not the honorable gentleman well know all this? There are certainly those who do, full well, know it all. I do not say this to reproach South Carolina. I only state the fact; and I think it will appear to be true, that among the earliest and boldest advocates of the tariff, as a measure of protection, and on the express ground of protection, were leading gentlemen of South Carolina in congress. I did not then, and can not now, understand their language in any other sense. * * *

Such, Mr. President, were the opinions of important and leading gentlemen from South Carolina, on the subject of internal improvement, in 1816. I went out of congress the next year, and, returning again in

1823, thought I found South Carolina where I had left her. I really supposed that all things remained as they were, and that the South Carolina doctrine of internal improvements would be defended by the same eloquent voices, and the same strong arms, as formerly. In the lapse of these six years, it is true, political associations had assumed a new aspect and new divisions. A strong party had risen in the south hostile to the doctrine of internal improvements, and had vigorously attacked that doctrine. Anticonsolidation was the flag under which this party fought; and its supporters inveighed against internal improvements, much after the manner in which the honorable gentleman has now inveighed against them, as part and parcel of the system of consolidation. Whether this party arose in South Carolina herself, or in her neighborhood, is more than I know. I think the latter. However that may have been, there were those found in South Carolina ready to make war upon it, and who did make intrepid war upon it. Names being regarded as things in such controversies, they bestowed on the anti-improvement gentlemen the appellation of radicals. Yes, sir, the appellation of radicals, as a term of distinction applicable and applied to those who denied the liberal doctrines of internal improvement, originated, according to the best of my recollection, somewhere between North Carolina and Georgia. Well, sir, these mischievous radicals were to be put down, and the strong arm of South Carolina was stretched out to put them down. About this time, sir, I returned to congress. The battle with the radicals had been fought, and our South Carolina champions of the doctrines of internal improvement had nobly maintained their ground, and were understood to have achieved a victory. We looked upon them as conquerors. They had driven back the enemy with discomfiture — a thing, by the way, sir, which is not always performed when it is promised.

(Mr. Webster quotes from a member from South Carolina who in a printed speech asserted that the system of internal improvements was first advocated by Mr. Calhoun. This opinion was held when Webster took his seat in congress and subsequently a bill authorizing the system in fact was voted for by South Carolina members; he followed that light till 1824. After an interruption by Mr. Calhoun to which he replies neatly, he proceeds: "I have thus * * * shown

if I am in error on the subject of internal improvement, how and in what company I fell into
that error. If I am wrong it is apparent who
misled me.")

On yet another point I was still more unac-
countably misunderstood. The gentleman
had harangued against "consolidation." I
told him, in reply, that there was one kind of
consolidation to which I was attached, and
that was the consolidation of our Union ; that
this was precisely that consolidation to which
I feared others were not attached ; that such
consolidation was the very end of the constitution, the leading object, as they had informed
us themselves, which its framers had kept in
view. I turned to their communication, and
read their very words, " The consolidation
of the Union," and expressed my devotion
to this sort of consolidation. I said, in terms,
that I wished not in the slightest degree
to augment the powers of this government ;
that my object was to preserve, not to enlarge ; and that by consolidating the Union
I understood no more than the strengthening
of the Union, and perpetuating it. Having
been thus explicit, having thus read from
the printed book the precise words which I

adopted, as expressing my own sentiments, it passes comprehension how any man could understand me as contending for an extension of the powers of the government, or for consolidation in that odious sense in which it means an accumulation, in the federal government, of the powers properly belonging to the states.

(The orator explains his position on the tariff question, which Hayne had claimed to be contradictory. He had voted against the tariff in 1824 but in 1828 he had merely voted to amend an existing law for the benefit of his constituents. He then dismisses the tariff question.)

Professing to be provoked by what he chose to consider a charge made by me against South Carolina, the honorable member, Mr. President, has taken up a new crusade against New England. Leaving altogether the subject of the public lands, in which his success, perhaps, had been neither distinguished nor satisfactory, and letting go, also, of the topic of the tariff, he sallied forth in a general assault on the opinions, politics, and parties of New England, as they have been exhibited in the last thirty years. This is natural. The "narrow policy" of the public lands had proved a legal settlement in South Carolina, and was not to be removed. The "accursed policy" of the tariff, also, had established the fact of its birth and parentage in the same state. No wonder, therefore, the gentleman wished to carry the war, as he expressed it, into the enemy's country. Prudently willing to quit these subjects, he was, doubtless, desirous of fastening on others which could not be transferred south of Mason and Dixon's line. The politics of New England became his theme; and it was in this part of his speech, I think, that he menaced me with sore discomfiture. Discomfiture! Why, sir, when he attacks anything which I maintain, and overthrows it, when he turns the right or left of any position which I take up, when he drives me from any ground I choose to occupy, he may then talk of discomfiture, but not till that distant day. What has he done? Has he maintained his own charges? Has he proved what he alleged? Has he sustained himself in his attack on the government, and on the history of the north, in the matter of the public lands? Has he disproved a fact, refuted a proposition, weakened an argument, maintained by me? Has he come within beat of drum of any position of mine? O, no; but he has "carried the war into the enemy's country!" Carried the war into the enemy's country! Yes, sir, and what sort of a war has he made of it? Why, sir, he has stretched a drag-net over the whole surface of perished pamphlets, indiscreet sermons, frothy paragraphs, and fuming popular addresses, over whatever the pulpit in its moments of alarm, the press in its heats, and parties in their extravagances, have severally thrown off in times of general excitement and violence. He has thus swept together a mass of such things as, but that they are now old and cold, the public health would have required him rather to leave in their state of dispersion. For a good long hour or two, we had the unbroken pleasure of listening to the honorable member, while he recited with his usual grace and spirit, and with evident high gusto, speeches, pamphlets, addresses, and all the *et ceteras* of the political press, such as warm heads produce in warm times, and such as it would be "discomfiture" indeed for any one whose taste did not delight in that sort of reading to be obliged to peruse. This is his war. This it is to carry war into the enemy's country. It is by an invasion of this sort that he flatters himself with the expectation of gaining laurels fit to adorn a senator's brow!

Mr. President, I shall not — it will not, I trust, be expected that I should — either now or at any time, separate this farrago into parts, and answer and examine its components. I shall hardly bestow upon it all a general re-mark or two. In the run of forty years, sir, under this constitution, we have experienced sundry successive violent party contests. Party arose, indeed, with the constitution itself, and, in some form or other, has attended it through the greater part of its history. Whether any other constitution than the old articles of con-federation was desirable, was itself a question on which parties formed; if a new constitu-tion were framed, what powers should be given to it was another question; and when it had been formed, what was, in fact, the just extent of the powers actually conferred was a third. Parties, as we know, existed under the first administration, as distinctly marked as those which have manifested themselves at any sub-sequent period. The contest immediately pre-ceding the political change in 1801, and that, again, which existed at the commencement of the late war, are other instances of party ex-citement, of something more than usual strength and intensity. In all these conflicts there was, no doubt, much of violence on both and all sides. It would be impossible, if one had a fancy for such employment, to adjust the relative *quantum* of violence between these contending parties. There was enough in each, as must always be expected in popular governments. With a great deal of proper and decorous discussion, there was mingled a great deal, also, of declamation, virulence, crimination, and abuse. In regard to any party, probably, at one of the leading epochs in the history of parties, enough may be found to make out another equally inflamed exhibition, as that with which the honorable member has edified us. For myself, sir, I shall not rake among the rubbish of bygone times, to see what I can find, or whether I cannot find something by which I can fix a blot on the escutcheon of any state, any party, or any part of the country. General Washington's administration was steadily and zealously maintained, as we all know, by New England. It was violently opposed elsewhere. We know in what quarter he had the most earnest, constant, and persevering support, in all his great and leading measures. We know where his private and personal character was held in the highest degree of attachment and veneration; and we know, too, where his measures were opposed, his services slighted, and his character vilified.

We know, or we might know if we turned to the journals, who expressed respect, gratitude and regret when he retired from the chief magistracy, and who refused to express either respect, gratitude or regret. I shall not open those journals. Publications more abusive or scurrilous never saw the light, than were sent forth against Washington, and all his leading measures, from presses south of New England. But I shall not look them up. I employ no scavengers; no one is in attendance on me, tendering such means of retaliation; and if there were, with an ass's load of them, with a bulk as huge as that which the gentleman himself has produced, I would not touch one of them. I see enough of the violence of our own times, to be no way anxious to rescue from forgetfulness the extravagances of times past.

Mr. President, in carrying his warfare, such as it is, into New England, the honorable gentleman all along professes to be acting on the defensive. He elects to consider me as having assailed South Carolina, and insists that he comes forth only as her champion, and in her defense. Sir, I do not admit that I made any attack whatever on South Carolina. Nothing like it. The honorable member, in his first speech, expressed opinions, in regard to revenue and some other topics, which I heard both with pain and with surprise. I told the gentleman I was aware that such sentiments were entertained *out* of the government, but had not expected to find them advanced in it; that I knew there were persons in the south who speak of our Union with indifference or doubt, taking pains to magnify its evils, and to say nothing of its benefits; that the honorable member himself, I was sure, could never be one of these; and I regretted the expression of such opinions as he had avowed, because I thought their obvious tendency was to encourage feelings of disrespect to the Union, and to weaken its connection. This, sir, is the sum and substance of all I said on the subject. And this constitutes the attack which called on the chivalry of the gentleman, in his own opinion, to harry us with such a foray among the party pamphlets and party proceedings of Massachusetts! If he means that I spoke with dissatisfaction or disrespect of the ebullitions of individuals in South Carolina, it is true. But if he means that I had assailed the character of the state, her honor or patriotism, that I had reflected on her history or her conduct, he has not the slightest ground for any such assumption. I did not even refer, I think, in my observations, to any collection of individuals. I said nothing of the recent conventions. I spoke in the most guarded and careful manner, and only expressed my regret for the publication of opinions which I presumed the honorable member disapproved as much as myself. In this, it seems, I was mistaken. I do not remember that the gentleman has disclaimed any sentiment, or any opinion, of a supposed anti-Union tendency, which on all or any of the recent occasions has been expressed. The whole drift of his speech has been rather to prove, that, in divers times and manners, sentiments equally liàble to my objection have been avowed in New England.

(Webster points out an inconsistency in Hayne's argument, and then questions the object of the Hartford convention, and shows the absurdity of charging the government of New England with the misinterpreted acts of an unauthorized convention.)

Then, sir, the gentleman has no fault to find with these recently promulgated South Carolina opinions. And certainly he need have none; for his own sentiments, as now advanced, and advanced on reflection, as far as I have been able to comprehend them, go the full length of all these opinions. I propose, sir, to say something on these, and to consider how far they are just and constitutional. Before doing that, however, let me observe that the eulogium pronounced on the character of the state of South Carolina, by the honorable gentleman, for her revolutionary and other merits, meets my hearty concurrence. I shall not acknowledge that the honorable member goes before me in regard for whatever of distinguished talent, or distinguished character, South Carolina has produced. I claim part of the honor, I partake in the pride, of her great names. I claim them for countrymen, one and all — the Laurenses, the Rutledges, the Pinckneys, the Sumters, the Marions, Americans all, whose fame is no more to be hemmed in by state lines, than their talents and patriotism were capable of being circumscribed within the same narrow limits. In their day and generation, they served and honored the country, and the whole country; and their renown is of the treasures of the whole country. Him whose honored name the gentleman himself bears [17] — does he esteem me less capable of gratitude for his patriotism, or sympathy for his sufferings, than if his eyes had first opened upon the light of Massachusetts, instead of South Carolina? Sir, does he suppose it in his power to exhibit a Carolina name so bright, as to produce envy in my bosom? No, sir; increased gratification and delight, rather. I thank God, that, if I am gifted with little of the spirit which is able to raise mortals to the skies, I have yet none, as I trust, of that other spirit, which would drag angels down. When I shall be found, sir, in my place here in the senate, or elsewhere, to sneer at public merit, because it happens to spring up beyond the little limits of my own state or neighborhood; when I refuse, for any such cause, or for any cause, the homage due to American talent, to elevated patriotism, to sincere devotion to liberty and the country; or, if I see an uncommon endowment of Heaven, if I see extraordinary capacity and virtue, in any son of the south, and if, moved

---

17. Isaac Hayne, great-uncle of Robert Y. Hayne, who was executed by the joint order of Colonel Balfour and Lord Rawdon. Hayne had taken the oath of allegiance to the British on condition that he should not be obliged to bear arms. He was forced into service; and on account of this broke his parole, and became an American officer. He was captured by the British and hanged.

by local prejudice or gangrened by state jealousy, I get up here to abate the tithe of a hair from his just character and just fame, may my tongue cleave to the roof of my mouth.

Sir, let me recur to pleasing recollections; let me indulge in refreshing remembrances of the past; let me remind you that, in early times, no states cherished greater harmony, both of principle and feeling, than Massachusetts and South Carolina. Would to God that harmony might again return! Shoulder to shoulder they went through the revolution; hand in hand they stood round the administration of Washington, and felt his own great arm lean on them for support. Unkind feeling, if it exists, alienation and distrust, are the growth, unnatural to such soils, of false principles since sown. They are weeds, the seeds of which that same great arm never scattered.

Mr. President, I shall enter on no encomium upon Massachusetts; she needs none. There she is. Behold her, and judge for yourselves. There is her history; the world knows it by heart. The past, at least, is secure. There is Boston, and Concord, and Lexington, and Bunker Hill; and there they will remain forever. The bones of her sons, fallen in the great struggle for independence, now lie mingled with the soil of every state from New England to Georgia; and there they will lie forever. And, sir, where American liberty raised its first voice, and where its youth was nurtured and sustained, there it still lives, in the strength of its manhood and full of its original spirit. If discord and disunion shall wound it, if party strife and blind ambition shall hawk at and tear it, if folly and madness, if uneasiness under salutary and necessary restraint, shall succeed in separating it from that Union, by which alone its existence is made sure, it will stand, in the end, by the side of that cradle in which its infancy was rocked; it will stretch forth its arm, with whatever of vigor it may still retain, over the friends who gather round it; and it will fall at last, if fall it must, amidst the proudest monuments of its own glory, and on the very spot of its origin.

There yet remains to be performed, Mr. President, by far the most grave and important duty which I feel to be devolved on me by this occasion. It is to state, and to defend, what I conceive to be the true principles of the constitution under which we are here assembled. I might well have desired that so weighty a task should have fallen into other and abler hands. I could have wished that it should have been executed by those whose character and experience give weight and influence to their opinions, such as cannot possibly belong to mine. But, sir, I have met the occasion, not sought it; and I shall proceed to state my own sentiments, without challenging for them any particular regard, with studied plainness, and as much precision as possible.

I understand the honorable gentleman from South Carolina to maintain that it is a right of the state legislatures to interfere, whenever, in their judgment, this government transcends its constitutional limits, and to arrest the operation of its laws.

I understand him to maintain this right as a right existing *under* the constitution, not as a right to overthrow it on the ground of extreme necessity, such as would justify violent revolution.

I understand him to maintain an authority, on the part of the states, thus to interfere, for the purpose of correcting the exercise of power by the general government, of checking it, and of compelling it to conform to their opinion of the extent of its powers,

THE NATIONAL CAPITOL, WASHINGTON

I understand him to maintain that the ultimate power of judging of the constitutional extent of its own authority is not lodged exclusively in the general government, or any branch of it; but that, on the contrary, the states may lawfully decide for themselves, and each state for itself, whether, in a given case, the act of the general government transcends its power.

I understand him to insist that, if the exigency of the case, in the opinion of any state government, require it, such state government may, by its own sovereign authority, annul an act of the general government which it deems plainly and palpably unconstitutional.

This is the sum of what I understand from him to be the South Carolina doctrine, and the doctrine which he maintains. I propose to consider it, and compare it with the constitution. Allow me to say, as a preliminary remark, that I call this the South Carolina doctrine only because the gentleman himself has so denominated it. I do not feel at liberty to say that South Carolina, as a state, has ever advanced these sentiments. I hope she has not, and never may. That a great majority of her people are opposed to the tariff laws, is doubtless true. That a majority, somewhat less than that just mentioned, conscientiously believe these laws unconstitutional, may probably also be true. But that any majority holds to the right of direct state interference at state discretion, the right of nullifying acts of congress by acts of state legislation, is more than I know, and what I shall be slow to believe.

That there are individuals besides the honorable gentleman who do maintain these opinions, is quite certain. I recollect the recent expression of a sentiment which circumstances attending its utterance and publication justify us in supposing was not unpremeditated: " The sovereignty of the state — never to be controlled, construed, or decided on, but by her own feelings of honorable justice. "

(Here occur two interruptions by Mr. Hayne, one in which he reads the resolution on which he relies for his authority. Webster contends that Hayne's interpretation of the resolution is incorrect. The latter explains that he contends for constitutional resistance. Webster is glad he does not misunderstand, and he does not admit the truth of the proposition; asserts that it cannot be maintained; admits an ultimate, violent remedy, that is, revolution; and denies that there is any mode in which a state, " as a member of the Union, can interfere and stop the progress of the general government by force of her own laws under any circumstances whatever.")

The inherent right in the people to reform their government I do not deny; and they have another right, and that is, to resist unconstitutional laws, without overturning the government. It is no doctrine of mine that unconstitutional laws bind the people. The great question is, Whose prerogative is it to decide on the constitutionality or unconstitutionality of the laws? On that, the main debate hinges.

This leads us to inquire into the origin of this government and the source of its power. Whose agent is it? Is it the creature of the state legislatures, or the creature of the people? If the government of the United States be the agent of the state governments, then they may control it, provided they can agree in the manner of controlling it; if it be the agent of the people, then the people alone can control it, restrain it, modify or reform it. It is observable enough, that the doctrine for which the honorable gentleman contends leads him to the necessity of maintaining, not only that this general government is the

creature of the states, but that it is , the
creature of each of the states severally, so
that each may assert the power for itself of
determining whether it acts within the limits
of its authority. It is the servant of four-
and-twenty masters, of different wills and
different purposes, and yet bound to obey
all. This absurdity (for it seems no less)
arises from a misconception as to the origin
of this government and its true character. It
is, sir, the people's constitution, the people's
government, made for the people, made by
the people, and answerable to the people.[18]
The people of the United States have declared
that this constitution shall be the supreme
law. We must either admit the proposition,
or dispute the authority. The states are,
unquestionably, sovereign, so far as their
sovereignty is not affected by this supreme
law. But the state legislatures, as political
bodies, however sovereign, are yet not
sovereign over the people. So far as the
people have given power to the general government, so far the grant is unquestionably
good, and the government holds of the peo-

---

18. Compare with the sentence in Lincoln's Gettsysburg address.
Theodore Parker uses the expression, "A government of all the people,
by all the people, for all the people."

ple, and not of the state governments. We are all agents of the same supreme power, the people. The general government and the state governments derive their authority from the same source. Neither can, in relation to the other, be called primary, though one is definite and restricted, and the other general and residuary. The national government possesses those powers which it can be shown the people have conferred on it, and no more. All the rest belongs to the state governments, or to the people themselves. So far as the people have restrained state sovereignty, by the expression of their will, in the constitution of the United States, so far, it must be admitted, state sovereignty is effectually controlled. I do not contend that it is, or ought to be, controlled farther. The sentiment to which I have referred propounds that state sovereignty is only to be controlled by its own "feeling of justice;" that is to say, it is not to be controlled at all, for one who is to follow his own feelings is under no legal control. Now, however men may think this ought to be, the fact is, that the people of the United States have chosen to impose control on state sovereignties. There are those, doubtless, who wish they had been left without restraint;

but the constitution has ordered the matter differently. To make war, for instance, is an exercise of sovereignty; but the constitution declares that no state shall make war. To coin money is another exercise of sovereign power; but no state is at liberty to coin money. Again, the constitution says that no sovereign state shall be so sovereign as to make a treaty. These prohibitions, it must be confessed, are a control on the state sovereignty of South Carolina, as well as of the other states, which does not arise "from her own feelings of honorable justice." Such an opinion, therefore, is in defiance of the plainest provisions of the constitution.

(The speaker contends that under the resolutions and constructions placed upon them by his opponents, the tariff laws are all such palpable usurpation as would justify the states in exercising their rights of nullification; supposes South Carolina so resolves but other states resolve differently; asks what power shall decide. He then points out the absurdity of the claim that South Carolina had no collision with the King's ministers in 1775, and asks contemptuously what now separates the state from Old England instead of from New England.)

Resolutions, sir, have been recently passed by the legislature of South Carolina. I need not refer to them; they go no farther than the honorable gentleman himself has gone, and I hope not so far. I content myself, therefore, with debating the matter with him.

And now, sir, what I have first to say on this subject is, that at no time, and under no circumstances, has New England, or any state in New England, or any respectable body of persons in New England, or any public man of standing in New England, put forth such a doctrine as this Carolina doctrine.

The gentleman has found no case, he can find none, to support his own opinions by New England authority. New England has studied the constitution in other schools, and under other teachers. She looks upon it with other regards, and deems more highly and reverently both of its just authority and its utility and excellence. The history of her legislative proceedings may be traced. The ephemeral effusions of temporary bodies, called together by the excitement of the occasion, may be hunted up; they have been hunted up. The opinions and votes of her public men, in and out of congress, may be explored. It will all be in vain. The Carolina doctrine can derive from her neither countenance nor support. She rejects it now; she always did reject it; and till she loses her senses, she always will reject it. The honorable member has referred to expressions on the subject of the embargo law, made in this place, by an honorable and venerable gentleman, now favoring us with his presence.[9] He quotes that distinguished senator with saying, that, in his judgment, the embargo law was unconstitutional, and that, therefore, in his opinion, the people were not bound to obey it. That, sir, is perfectly constitutional language. An unconstitutional law is not binding; *but then it does not rest with a resolution or a law of a state legislature to decide whether an act of congress be or be not constitutional.* An unconstitutional act of congress would not bind the people of this district, although they have no legislature to interfere in their behalf; and, on the other hand, a constitutional law of congress does bind the citizens of every state, although all their legislatures should undertake to annul it by act or resolution. The venerable Connecticut senator is a constitutional lawyer, of sound principles and enlarged knowledge: a statesman practiced and experi-

19. Mr. Hillhouse, of Connecticut.

enced, bred in the company of Washington, and holding just views upon the nature of our governments. He believed the embargo unconstitutional, and so did others; but what then? Who did he suppose was to decide that question? The state legislatures? Certainly not. No such sentiment ever escaped his lips.

Let us follow up, sir, this New England opposition to the embargo laws; let us trace it, till we discern the principle which controlled and governed New England throughout the whole course of that opposition. We shall then see what similarity there is between the New England school of constitutional opinions and this modern Carolina school. The gentleman, I think, read a petition from some single individual, addressed to the legislature of Massachusetts, asserting the Carolina doctrine; that is, the right of state interference to arrest the laws of the Union. The fate of that petition shows the sentiment of the legislature. It met no favor. The opinions of Massachusetts were otherwise. They had been expressed in 1798,[20] in answer to the

---

20. The Virginia resolutions were passed by the legislature of that state in 1798, in antagonism to the loose construction views of the Federalists. The resolutions declared the Union to be a compact, each party to which had a right to "interpose," in order to protect and defend itself against any infringements of the compact.

resolutions of Virginia, and she did not depart from them, nor bend them to the times. Misgoverned, wronged, oppressed, as she felt herself to be, she still held fast her integrity to the Union. The gentleman may find in her proceedings much evidence of dissatisfaction with the measures of government, and great and deep dislike to the embargo; all this makes the case so much the stronger for her; for, notwithstanding all this dissatisfaction and dislike, she claimed no right, still, to sever asunder the bonds of the Union. There was heat and there was anger in her political feeling. Be it so; her heat or her anger did not, nevertheless, betray her into infidelity to the government. The gentleman labors to prove that she disliked the embargo as much as South Carolina dislikes the tariff, and expressed her dislike as strongly. Be it so; but did she propose the Carolina remedy? did she threaten to interfere, by state authority, to annul the laws of the Union? That is the question for the gentleman's consideration.

No doubt, sir, a great majority of the people of New England conscientiously believed the embargo law of 1807 unconstitutional; as conscientiously, certainly, as the people of South Carolina hold that opinion of the tariff. They

reasoned thus: Congress has power to regulate commerce; but here is a law, they said,
stopping all commerce and stopping it in-
definitely. The law is perpetual; that is, it is
not limited in point of time, and must of
course continue until it shall be repealed by
some other law. It is as perpetual, therefore, as the law against treason or murder.
Now is this regulating commerce, or destroying it? Is it guiding, controlling, giving the
rule to commerce, as a subsisting thing, or is
it putting an end to it altogether? Nothing
is more certain, than that a majority in New
England deemed this law a violation of the
constitution. The very case required by the
gentleman to justify state interference had
then arisen. Massachusetts believed this law
to be "a deliberate, palpable, and dangerous
exercise of a power not granted by the constitution." Deliberate it was, for it was long
continued; palpable she thought it, as no
words in the constitution gave the power,
and only a construction, in her opinion most
violent, raised it; dangerous it was, since it
threatened utter ruin to her most important
interests. Here, then, was a Carolina case.
How did Massachusetts deal with it? It was,
as she thought, a plain, manifest, palpable

violation of the constitution, and it brought ruin to her doors. Thousands of families, and hundreds of thousands of individuals, were beggared by it. While she saw and felt all this, she saw and felt also, that, as a measure of national policy, it was perfectly futile; that the country was no way benefited by that which caused so much individual distress; that it was efficient only for the production of evil, and all that evil inflicted on ourselves. In such a case, under such circumstances, how did Massachusetts demean herself? Sir, she remonstrated, she memorialized, she addressed herself to the general government, not exactly " with the concentrated energy of passion," but with her own strong sense and the energy of sober conviction. But she did not interpose the arm of her own power to arrest the law and break the embargo. Far from it. Her principles bound her to two things; and she followed her principles, lead where they might. First, to submit to every constitutional law of congress, and secondly, if the constitutional validity of the law be doubted, to refer that question to the decision of the proper tribunals. The first principle is vain and ineffectual without the second. A majority of us in New England believed the embargo law unconstitutional; but the great question was, and always will be in such cases, Who is to decide this? Who is to judge between the people and the government? And, sir, it is quite plain that the constitution of the United States confers on the government itself, to be exercised by its appropriate department, and under its own responsibility to the people, this power of deciding ultimately and conclusively upon the just extent of its own authority. If this had not been done, we should not have advanced a single step beyond the old confederation.

Being fully of opinion that the embargo law was unconstitutional, the people of New England were yet equally clear in the opinion —it was a matter they did not doubt upon— that the question, after all, must be decided by the judicial tribunals of the United States. Before these tribunals, therefore, they brought the question. Under the provisions of the law, they had given bonds to millions in amount, and which were alleged to be forfeited. They suffered the bonds to be sued, and thus raised the question. In the old-fashioned way of settling disputes, they went to law. The case came to hearing and solemn argument; and he who espoused their cause,

and stood up for them against the validity of
the embargo act, was none other than that
great man, of whom the gentleman has made
honorable mention, Samuel Dexter.[21] He
was then, sir, in the fullness of his knowledge,
and the maturity of his strength. He had
retired from long and distinguished public service here, to the renewed pursuit of professional duties, carrying with him all that en-
largement and expansion, all the new strength
and force, which an acquaintance with the
more general subjects discussed in the national
councils is capable of adding to professional
attainment, in a mind of true greatness and
comprehension. He was a lawyer, and he
was also a statesman. He had studied the
constitution, when he filled public station,
that he might defend it. He had examined
its principles that he might maintain them.
More than all men, or at least as much as
any man, he was attached to the general government and to the union of the states. His
feelings and opinions all ran in that direction.
A question of constitutional law, too, was, of
all subjects, that one which was best suited to

---

21. Samuel Dexter was a noted Massachusetts lawyer. He was suc-
cessively, for short periods, secretary of war and secretary of the treasury
in the cabinet of President John Adams.

his talents and learning. Aloof from techni-
cality, and unfettered by artificial rule, such a
question gave opportunity for that deep and
clear analysis, that mighty grasp of principle,
which so much distinguished his higher efforts.
His very statement was argument; his infer-
ence seemed demonstration. The earnestness
of his own conviction wrought conviction in
others. One was convinced, and believed,
and assented, because it was gratifying, delightful, to think, and feel, and believe, in
unison with an intellect of such evident superiority.

Mr. Dexter, sir, such as I have described
him, argued the New England cause. He
put into his effort his whole heart, as well as
all the powers of his understanding; for he
had avowed, in the most public manner, his
entire concurrence with his neighbors on the
point in dispute. He argued the cause; it
was lost, and New England submitted. The
established tribunals pronounced the law constitutional, and New England acquiesced.
Now, sir, is not this the exact opposite of the
doctrine of the gentleman from South Carolina? According to him, instead of referring
to the judicial tribunals, we should have
broken up the embargo by laws of our own;

we should have repealed it, *quoad*[22] New England ; for we had a strong, palpable, and oppressive case.   Sir, we believed the embargo unconstitutional; but still that was matter of opinion, and who was to decide it? We thought it a clear case; but, nevertheless, we did not take the law into our own hands, because we did not wish to bring about a revolution, nor to break up the Union; for I maintain, that between submission to the decision of the constituted tribunals, and revolution, or disunion, there is no middle ground; there is no ambiguous condition, half allegiance and half rebellion.   And, sir, how futile, how very futile it is, to admit the right of state interference, and then attempt to save it from the character of unlawful resistance by adding terms of qualification to the causes and occasions, leaving all these qualifications, like the case itself, in the discretion of the state governments!   It must be a clear case, it is said, a deliberate case, a palpable case, a dangerous case.   But then the state is still left at liberty to decide for herself what is clear, what is deliberate, what is palpable, what is dangerous.   Do adjectives and epithets avail anything ?

---

22. To the extent of New England.

Sir, the human mind is so constituted, that the merits of both sides of a controversy appear very clear, and very palpable, to those who respectively espouse them; and both sides usually grow clearer as the controversy advances. South Carolina sees unconstitutionality in the tariff; she sees oppression there, also, and she sees danger. Pennsylvania, with a vision not less sharp, looks at the same tariff, and sees no such thing in it; she sees it all constitutional, all useful, all safe. The faith of South Carolina is strengthened by opposition, and she now not only sees, but *resolves*, that the tariff is palpably unconstitutional, oppressive, and dangerous; but Pennsylvania, not to be behind her neighbors, and equally willing to strengthen her own faith by a confident asseration, *resolves*, also, and gives to every warm affirmative of South Carolina a plain, downright, Pennsylvania negative. South Carolina, to show the strength and unity of her opinion, brings her assembly to a unanimity, within seven voices; Pennsylvania, not to be outdone in this respect any more than in others, reduces her dissentient fraction to a single vote. Now, sir, again, I ask the gentleman, What is to be done? Are these states both right? Is he bound to consider them both right? If not, which is in the wrong? or rather, which has the best right to decide? And if he, and if I, are not to know what the constitution means, and what it is, till those two state legislatures, and the twenty-two others, shall agree in its construction, what have we sworn to, when we have sworn to maintain it! I was forcibly struck, sir, with one reflection, as the gentleman went on in his speech. He quoted Mr. Madison's resolutions, to prove that a state may interfere, in a case of deliberate, palpable, and dangerous exercise of a power not granted. The honorable member supposes the tariff law to be such an exercise of power; and that consequently a case has arisen in which the state may, if it see fit, interfere by its own law. Now it so happens, nevertheless, that Mr. Madison deems this same tariff law quite constitutional. Instead of a clear and palpable violation, it is, in his judgment, no violation at all. So that, while they use his authority for a hypothetical case, they reject it in the very case before them. All this, sir, shows the inherent futility, I had almost said a stronger word, of conceding this power of interference to the states, and then attempting to secure it from abuse by imposing qualifications of which the states themselves are to judge. One of two things is true; either the laws of the Union are beyond the discretion and beyond the control of the states, or else we have no constitution of general government, and are thrust back again to the days of the confederation.

Let me here say, sir, that if the gentleman's doctrine had been received and acted upon in New England, in the times of the embargo and non-intercourse, we should probably not now have been here. The government would very likely have gone to pieces, and crumbled into dust. No stronger case can ever arise than existed under those laws; no states can ever entertain a clearer conviction than the New England states then entertained; and if they had been under the influence of that heresy of opinion, as I must call it, which the honorable member espouses, this Union would, in all probability, have been scattered to the four winds. I ask the gentleman, therefore, to apply his principles to that case; I ask him to come forth and declare, whether, in his opinion, the New England states would have been justified in interfering to break up the embargo system under the conscientious opinions which they held upon it. Had they a right to annul that law, does he admit or deny? If what is thought palpably unconstitutional in South Carolina justifies that state in arresting the progress of the law, tell me whether that which was thought palpably unconstitutional also in Massachusetts would have justified her in doing the same thing. Sir, I deny the whole doctrine. It has not a foot of ground in the constitution to stand on. No public man of reputation ever advanced it in Massachusetts in the warmest times, or could maintain himself upon it there at any time. * * *

I must now beg to ask, sir, Whence is this supposed right of the states derived? Where do they find the power to interfere with the laws of the Union? Sir, the opinion which the honorable gentleman maintains is a notion founded in a total misapprehension, in my judgment, of the origin of this government, and of the foundation on which it stands. I hold it to be a popular government, erected by the people; those who administer it, responsible to the people; and itself capable of being amended and modified, just as the people may choose it should be. It is as popular, just as truly emanating from the people, as the state governments. It is created for one purpose; the state governments for another. It has its own powers; they have theirs. There is no more authority with them to arrest the operation of a law of congress, than with congress to arrest the operation of their laws. We are here to administer a constitution emanating immediately from the people, and trusted by them to our administration. It is not the creature of the state governments. It is of no moment to the argument that certain acts of the state legislatures are necessary to fill our seats in this body. That is not one of their original state powers, a part of the sovereignty of the state. It is a duty which the people, by the constitution itself, have imposed on the state legislatures, and which they might have left to be performed elsewhere, if they had seen fit. So they have left the choice of president with electors; but all this does not affect the proposition that this whole government — president, senate, and house of representatives — is a popular government. It leaves it still all its popular character. The governor of the state (in some of the states) is chosen, not directly by the people, but by those who are chosen by the people for the purpose of performing, among other duties, that of electing a goveruor. Is the government of the state, on that account, not a popular government? This government, sir, is the independent offspring of the popular will. It is not the creature of state legislatures; nay, more, if the whole truth must be told, the people brought it into existence, established it, and have hitherto supported it, for the very purpose, amongst others, of imposing certain salutary restraints on state sovereignties. The states cannot now make war; they cannot contract alliances; they cannot make, each for itself, separate regulations of commerce; they cannot lay imposts; they cannot coin money. If this constitution, sir, be the creature of state legislatures, it must be admitted that it has obtained a strange control over the volition of its creators.

The people, then, sir, erected this government. They gave it a constitution, and in that constitution they have enumerated the powers which they bestow on it. They have made it a limited government. They have defined its authority. They have restrained it to the exercise of such powers as are granted; and all others, they declare, are reserved to the states or the people. But, sir, they have not stopped here. If they had, they would have accomplished but half their work. No definition can be so clear, as to avoid possibility of doubt; no limitation so precise, as to exclude all uncertainty. Who, then, shall construe this grant of the people? Who shall interpret their will, where it may be supposed they have left it doubtful? With whom do they repose this ultimate right of deciding on the powers of the government? Sir, they have settled all this in the fullest manner. They have left it with the government itself, in its appropriate branches. Sir, the very chief end, the main design, for which the whole constitution was framed and adopted, was to establish a government that should not be obliged to act through state agency, or depend on state opinion and state discretion. The people had had quite enough of that kind of government under the confederacy. Under that system, the legal action, the application of law to individuals, belonged exclusively to the states. Congress could only recommend; their acts were not of binding force till the states had adopted and sanctioned them. Are we in that condition still? Are we yet at the mercy of state discretion and state construction? Sir, if we are, then vain will be our attempt to maintain the constitution under which we sit.

But, sir, the people have wisely provided,

in the constitution itself, a proper, suitable mode and tribunal for settling questions of constitutional law. There are in the constitution grants of powers to congress, and restrictions on those powers. There are, also, prohibitions on the states. Some authority must, therefore, necessarily exist, having the ultimate jurisdiction to fix and ascertain the interpretation of these grants, restrictions, and prohibitions. The constitution has itself pointed out, ordained, and established that authority. How has it accomplished this great and essential end? By declaring, sir, that *"the constitution, and the laws of the United States made in pursuance thereof, shall be the supreme law of the land, anything in the constitution or laws of any state to the contrary notwithstanding."* [23]

This, sir, was the first great step. By this the supremacy of the constitution and laws of the United States is declared. The people so will it. No state law is to be valid which comes in conflict with the constitution, or any law of the United States passed in pursuance of it. But who shall decide this question of interference? To whom lies the last appeal? This, sir, the constitution itself decides also,

---

23. Constitution of the United States, Art. VI, Clause 2.

by declaring "*that the judicial power shall extend to all cases arising under the constitution and laws of the United States.*"[24] These two provisions, sir, cover the whole ground. They are, in truth, the keystone of the arch! With these it is a government; without them it is a confederacy. In pursuance of these clear and express provisions, congress established, at its very first session, in the judicial act, a mode for carrying them into full effect, and for bringing all questions of constitutional power to the final decision of the supreme court. It then, sir, became a government. It then had the means of self-protection; and but for this, it would, in all probability, have been now among the things which are past. Having constituted the government, and declared its powers, the people have further said, that, since somebody must decide on the extent of these powers, the government shall itself decide; subject, always, like other popular governments, to its responsibility to the people. And now, sir, I repeat, how is it that a state legislature acquires any power to interfere? Who, or what, gives them the right to say to the people, "We, who are your agents and servants, for one purpose, will undertake

---

24. Constitution of the United States, Art. III, Sec. II, Clause 1.

to decide that your other agents and servants, appointed by you for another purpose, have transcended the authority you gave them"? The reply would be, I think, not impertinent, — "Who made you a judge over another's servants? To their own masters they stand or fall."

Sir, I deny this power of state legislatures altogether. It cannot stand the test of examination. Gentlemen may say, that, in an extreme case, a state government might protect the people from intolerable oppression. Sir, in such a case, the people might protect themselves, without the aid of the state governments. Such a case warrants revolution. It must make, when it comes, a law for itself. A nullifying act of a state legislature cannot alter the case, nor make resistance any more lawful. In maintaining these sentiments, sir, I am but asserting the rights of the people. I state what they have declared, and insist on their right to declare it. They have chosen to repose this power in the general government, and I think it my duty to support it, like other constitutional powers.

For myself, sir, I do not admit the jurisdiction of South Carolina, or any other state, to prescribe my constitutional duty, or to

A VIEW DOWN PENNSYLVANIA AVENUE, WASHINGTON

settle, between me and the people, the validity of laws of congress for which I have voted. I decline her umpirage. I have not sworn to support the constitution according to her construction of its clauses. I have not stipulated, by my oath of office or otherwise, to come under any responsibility, except to the people, and those whom they have appointed to pass upon the question, whether laws supported by my votes conform to the constitution of the country. And, sir, if we look to the general nature of the case, could anything have been more preposterous, than to make a government for the whole Union, and yet leave its powers subject, not to one interpretation, but to thirteen or twenty-four interpretations? Instead of one tribunal, established by all, responsible to all, with power to decide for all, shall constitutional questions be left to four-and-twenty popular bodies, each at liberty to decide for itself, and none bound to respect the decisions of others; and each at liberty, too, to give a new construction on every new election of its own members? Would anything with such a principle in it, or rather with such a destitution of all principle, be fit to be called a government? No, sir. It should not be denominated a constitution. It should be called, rather, a collection of topics for ever-lasting controversy; heads of debate for a disputatious people. It would not be a government. It would not be adequate to any practical good, or fit for any country to live under.

To avoid all possibility of being misunderstood, allow me to repeat again, in the fullest manner, that I claim no powers for the government by forced or unfair construction. I admit that it is a government of strictly limited powers; of enumerated, specified, and particularized powers; and that whatsoever is not granted, is withheld. But notwithstanding all this, and however the grant of powers may be expressed, its limit and extent may yet, in some cases, admit of doubt; and the general government would be good for nothing, it would be incapable of long existing, if some mode had not been provided in which those doubts, as they should arise, might be peaceably but authoritatively solved.

And now, Mr. President, let me run the honorable gentleman's doctrine a little into its practical application. Let us look at his probable *modus operandi*.[25] If a thing can be done, an ingenious man can tell *how* it is to

25 Mode of operation.

be done.   Now I wish to be informed *how*
this state interference is to be put in practice,
without violence, bloodshed, and rebellion.
We will take the existing case of the tariff
law.   South Carolina is said to have made up
her opinion upon it.   If we do not repeal it, (as
we probably shall not,) she will then apply to
the case the remedy of her doctrine.   She
will, we must suppose, pass a law of her legislature, declaring the several acts of congress,
usually called the tariff laws, null and void, so
far as they respect South Carolina, or the
citizens thereof.   So far, all is a paper trans-
action, and easy enough.   But the collector
at Charleston is collecting the duties imposed
by these tariff laws.   He, therefore, must be
stopped.   The collector will seize the goods if
the tariff duties are not paid.   The state
authorities will undertake their rescue; the
marshal, with his posse, will come to the
collector's aid, and here the contest begins.
The militia of the state will be called out to
sustain the nullifying act.   They will march,
sir, under a very gallant leader; for I believe
the honorable member himself commands the
militia of that part of the state.   He will
raise the NULLIFYING ACT on his standard,
and spread it out as his banner !   It will have

a preamble, bearing that the tariff laws are palpable, deliberate, and dangerous violations of the constitution! He will proceed, with his banner flying, to the custom-house in Charleston,

> "All the while,
> Sonorous metal blowing martial sounds."

Arrived at the custom-house, he will tell the collector that he must collect no more duties under any of the tariff laws. This he will be somewhat puzzled to say, by the way, with a grave countenance, considering what hand South Carolina herself had in that of 1816. But, sir, the collector would not, probably, desist at his bidding. He would show him the law of congress, the treasury instruction, and his own oath of office. He would say, he should perform his duty, come what might.

Here would come a pause; for they say that a certain stillness precedes the tempest. The trumpeter would hold his breath awhile, and before all this military array should fall on the custom-house, collector, clerks, and all, it is very probable some of those composing it would request of their gallant commander-in-chief to be informed a little upon the point of law; for they have, doubtless, a just respect for his opinions as a lawyer, as well as for his bravery as a soldier. They know he has read Blackstone[26] and the constitution, as well as Turenne[27] and Vauban.[28] They would ask him, therefore, something concerning their rights in this matter. They would inquire, whether it was not somewhat dangerous to resist a law of the United States. What would be the nature of their offense, they would wish to learn, if they, by military force and array, resisted the execution in Carolina of a law of the United States, and it should turn out, after all, that the law *was constitutional?* He would answer, of course, treason. No lawyer could give any other answer. John Fries,[29] he would tell them, had learned that, some years ago. How, then, they would ask, do you propose to defend us? We are not afraid of bullets, but treason has a way of taking people off that we do not much relish. How do you propose to defend us? " Look at my floating banner," he would reply; " see there the *nullifying law !* " Is it your opinion, gallant commander, they would then say, that,

26. Eminent English law commentator — 1723.
27. Writer and soldier. Marshal of France in 1644.
28. Famous French military engineer — 1633-1707.
29. A German of Eastern Pennsylvania who opposed the collection of taxes levied upon his house, incited riot and was tried for treason, 1799.

if we should be indicted for treason, that same floating banner of yours would make a good plea in bar? "South Carolina is a sovereign state," he would reply. That is true; but would the judge admit our plea? "These tariff laws," he would repeat, "are unconstitutional, palpably, deliberately, dangerously." That may all be so; but if the tribunal should not happen to be of that opinion, shall we swing for it? We are ready to die for our country, but it is rather an awkward business, this dying without touching the ground! After all, that is a sort of hemp tax worse than any part of the tariff.

Mr. President, the honorable gentleman would be in a dilemma, like that of another great general. He would have a knot [30] before him which he could not untie. He must cut it with his sword. He must say to his followers, "Defend yourselves with your bayonets;" and this is war — civil war.

Direct collision, therefore, between force and force, is the unavoidable result of that remedy for the revision of unconstitutional

---

30. Gordius was a peasant who became king of Phrygia. An oracle declared that whoever untied the knot by which the yoke was tied to his wagon would be made ruler of the world. Alexander tried and not succeeding cut the knot with his sword.

laws which the gentleman contends for. It must happen in the very first case to which it is applied. Is not this the plain result? To resist by force the execution of a law, generally, is treason. Can the courts of the United States take notice of the indulgence of a state to commit treason? The common saying that a state cannot commit treason herself, is nothing to the purpose. Can she authorize others to do it? If John Fries had produced an act of Pennsylvania, annulling the law of congress, would it have helped his case? Talk about it as we will, these doctrines go the length of revolution. They are incompatible with any peaceable administration of the government. They lead directly to disunion and civil commotion; and therefore it is, that at their commencement, when they are first found to be maintained by respectable men, and in a tangible form, I enter my public protest against them all.

The honorable gentleman argues, that if this government be the sole judge of the extent of its own powers, whether that right of judging be in congress or the supreme court, it equally subverts state sovereignty. This the gentleman sees, or thinks he sees, although he cannot perceive how the right of judging, in this matter, if left to the exercise of state legislatures, has any tendency to subvert the government of the Union. The gentleman's opinion may be, that the right *ought not* to have been lodged with the general government; he may like better such a constitution as we should have under the right of state interference; but I ask him to meet me on the plain matter of fact. I ask him to meet me on the constitution itself. I ask him if the power is not found there, clearly and visibly found there?

But, sir, what is this danger, and what are the grounds of it? Let it be remembered that the constitution of the United States is not unalterable. It is to continue in its present form no longer than the people who established it shall choose to continue it. If they shall become convinced that they have made an injudicious or inexpedient partition and distribution of power between the state governments and the general government, they can alter that distribution at will.

If anything be found in the national constitution, either by original provision or subsequent interpretation, which ought not to be in it, the people know how to get rid of it. If any construction be established unacceptable to them, so as to become practically a part of the constitution, they will amend it, at their own sovereign pleasure. But while the people choose to maintain it as it is, while they are satisfied with it, and refuse to change it, who has given, or who can give, to the state legislatures a right to alter it, either by interference, construction, or otherwise? Gentlemen do not seem to recollect that the people have any power to do anything for themselves. They imagine there is no safety for them, any longer than they are under the close guardianship of the state legislatures. Sir, the people have not trusted their safety, in regard to the general constitution, to these hands. They have required other security, and taken other bonds. They have chosen to trust themselves, first, to the plain words of the instrument, and to such construction as the government itself, in doubtful cases, should put on its own powers, and under their oaths of office, and subject to their responsibility to them; just as the people of a state trust their own state government with a similar power. Secondly, they have reposed their trust in the efficacy of frequent elections, and in their own power to remove their own servants and agents whenever they see cause.   Thirdly, they have reposed trust in the judicial power, which, in order that it might be trustworthy, they have made as respectable, as disinterested, and as independent as was practicable.   Fourthly, they have seen fit to rely, in case of necessity, or high expediency, on their known and admitted power to alter or amend the constitution, peaceably and quietly, whenever experience shall point out defects or imperfections.   And, finally, the people of the United States have at no time, in no way, directly or indirectly, authorized any state legislature to construe or interpret *their* high instrument of government; much less, to interfere, by their own power, to arrest its course and operation.

If, sir, the people in these respects had done otherwise than they have done, their constitution could neither have been preserved, nor would it have been worth preserving.   And if its plain provisions shall now be disregarded, and these new doctrines interpolated in it, it will become as feeble and helpless a being as its enemies, whether early or more recent, could possibly desire.   It will exist in every state, but as a poor dependent on state permission.   It must borrow leave to be, and will be no longer than state pleasure, or state discretion, sees fit to grant the indulgence, and prolong its poor existence.

But, sir, although there are fears, there are hopes also. The people have preserved this, their own chosen constitution, for forty years, and have seen their happiness, prosperity, and renown grow with its growth, and strengthen with its strength. They are now, generally, strongly attached to it. Over-thrown by direct assault, it cannot be; evaded, undermined, NULLIFIED, it will not be, if we, and those who shall succeed us here, as agents and representatives of the people, shall conscientiously and vigilantly discharge the two great branches of our public trust — faithfully to preserve, and wisely to administer it.

Mr. President, I have thus stated the reasons of my dissent to the doctrines which have been advanced and maintained. I am conscious of having detained you and the senate much too long. I was drawn into the debate with no previous deliberation, such as is suited to the discussion of so grave and important a subject. But it is a subject of which my heart is full, and I have not been willing to suppress the utterance of its spontaneous sentiments. I can not, even now, persuade

myself to relinquish it, without expressing
once more my deep conviction, that, since it
respects nothing less than the Union of the
states, it is of most vital and essential importance to the public happiness. I profess, sir,
in my career hitherto, to have kept steadily
in view the prosperity and honor of the whole
country, and the preservation of our federal
Union. It is to that Union we owe our safety
at home, and our consideration and dignity
abroad. It is to that Union that we are
chiefly indebted for whatever makes us most
proud of our country. That Union we
reached only by the discipline of our virtues
in the severe school of adversity. It had its
origin in the necessities of disordered finance,
prostrate commerce, and ruined credit.
Under its benign influences, these great
interests immediately awoke, as from the
dead, and sprang forth with newness of life.
Every year of its duration has teemed with
fresh proofs of its utility and its blessings; and
although our territory has stretched out wider
and wider, and our population spread farther
and farther, they have not outrun its protection
or its benefits. It has been to us all a copious
fountain of national, social, and personal happiness.

I have not allowed myself, sir, to look beyond the Union, to see what might lie hidden in the dark recess behind. I have not coolly weighed the chances of preserving liberty when the bonds that unite us together shall be broken asunder. I have not accustomed myself to hang over the precipice of disunion, to see whether, with my short sight, I can fathom the depth of the abyss below; nor could I regard him as a safe counselor in the affairs of this government, whose thoughts should be mainly bent on considering, not how the Union should be best preserved, but how tolerable might be the condition of the people when it shall be broken up and destroyed. While the Union lasts, we have high, exciting, gratifying prospects spread out before us, for us and our children. Beyond that I seek not to penetrate the veil. God grant that in my day, at least, that curtain may not rise! God grant that on my vision never may be opened what lies behind! When my eyes shall be turned to behold for the last time the sun in heaven, may I not see him shining on the broken and dishonored fragments of a once glorious Union; on states dissevered, discordant, belligerent; on a land rent with civil feuds, or drenched, it may be, in fraternal blood!   Let their last feeble and lingering glance rather behold the gorgeous ensign of the republic, now known and honored throughout the earth, still full high advanced, its arms and trophies streaming in their original luster, not a stripe erased or polluted, not a single star obscured, bearing for its motto no such miserable interrogatory as "What is all this worth?" nor those other words of delusion and folly, "Liberty first and Union afterwards;" but everywhere, spread all over in characters of living light, blazing on all its ample folds, as they float over the sea and over the land, and in every wind under the whole heavens, that other sentiment, dear to every true American heart — Liberty *and* Union, now and forever, one and inseparable!

After Webster had completed his speech Hayne rose for a rejoinder and argued the constitutional question.   His chief contention was that the constitution is a compact between the states, that a contract between two with one only possessing the power of interpretation would mean the practical surrender to that one of all the power, therefore the general government does not possess the authority to construe its own powers — at least such is Webster's statement of the case.   In reply Mr. Webster showed the absurdity of making the thing created, that is, the government, a party to the compact that created it. Then granting for purposes of argument that the government is in the nature of a compact he proceeds to show that the only way to determine the powers of the compact is by a study and construction of its terms. Then he finds in the constitution that the laws passed by Congress in pursuance of the constitution shall be the supreme law of the land and that the judicial power of the United States shall extend to every case arising under the laws of congress. This is conclusive and forever settles the unconstitutionality of the doctrine of state rights.

Studies

Structure

The great length of the *Reply* will prevent your making so close an outline as was presented for Lincoln's *Gettysburg Address*, but you should make the outline full for the direct argument by which Webster disposes of the dogma of State Rights. Note the personal matters of the introduction and the various secondary questions he reviews and then omitting these from further consideration reduce to writing the argument of his plea. It will not be the easiest task but you will succeed. You may find yourself making several copies before one satisfies you perfectly but that is no more than every person must do who studies under even the best personal tuition.

When you have prepared the outline and are sure you have all the points of the argument, reduce them to the fewest possible words and then make a final copy in form like the one of the *Gettysburg Address* on page 26. This will enable you to see the whole argument at a glance and will show you something of the way in which the thoughts lay in the mind of Webster before he clothed them in words.

You will arrange the matter of your outline under the three great headings : *Introduction, Dis-*

cussion, and *Conclusion.* The introduction in the speech ends just before the paragraph beginning " I spoke, sir, of the ordinance of 1787." Where does the conclusion begin? How many distinct lines of argument do you find Webster pursuing in the body of the speech? Is the transition from one to another of these logical and natural? Could any of them be omitted as irrelevant? Are you impressed with the unity, the *oneness* of the oration? How many readings are required for you to get in mind the full course of the argument?

Thought

As an oration that ranks among the most powerful ever delivered, the *Reply to Hayne* deserves close and particular study. The profound principles discussed can be appreciated only through thorough understanding of the details and minor phases of the thought. To get in all cases Webster's full and exact meaning, first look up in a good dictionary every unfamiliar word. Perhaps the term *farrago* (page 87, line 3) is new to you. You must understand that it means *a confused mixture, a jumble,* in order to feel fully Webster's contempt for the mass of printed matter brought to light by his opponent. Again, consider the words *vilified* (page 88, last line) and *scurrilous* (page 89, ¶ 1). How much is added to the context if one knows, not, in a vague way, that these terms indicate baseness, but definitely, that *vilify* means *to make base in the sight of others*, usually as an unjustifiable gratification of low and bitter feeling, and that *scurrilous* could be applied only to "publications" which are unfair and which express ill-feeling. Likewise, it is not enough to guess or know vaguely that the word *encomium* (page 94, ¶ 3) means *praise;* it indicates *strong commendation* and the reader must realize this if he is to share the orator's feeling. An attempt to find not only the general definition but the finer shades of meaning of every other word not well understood will be amply repaid.

Webster in several cases adds zest to his oration by the use of vigorous figures of speech. He begins, indeed, with likening the course of the discussion in the senate to that of the mariner who, driven out of his way on a stormy sea, seizes his first opportunity to take his bearings. Can you think of a more effective means of impressing the need of returning to the original point of the discussion that the exact position in the debate might be realized? Notice the amusing metaphor which runs through pages 45, 46 and 47. What effect do you suppose it had upon the audience? Trace carefully the application of all other figures that you find. Read aloud slowly and carefully the last paragraph of the oration, since it is filled with powerful and vivid figures.

The speech abounds in allusions. Many of these references are explained in the notes.

Satisfy yourself of the meaning of all others before you leave your study of the speech. Get clearly in mind the meaning of State Sovereignty and Nullification and the attitude of both South Carolina and New England toward the public lands discussion and the interpretation of the Constitution.

Sometimes single sentences demand particular notice because of peculiar meaning and force. For example, on page 76, the meaning of the sentence, "The harvest of neutrality was great but we have gathered it all," may not be at once evident. It may require particular consideration to bring out the idea that *while the nations of Europe were at war, American ships sailing under a neutral flag reaped great advantages from trade, but such a condition is now past.* Again on page 80, line 4, the sentence, "The tariff of 1816 — South Carolina votes," calls for especial attention. Note the effect of the use of one of the enemy's own weapons. Sentences like these cannot be slighted if a clear understanding of the essay in its entirety is to be gained.

Read the paragraph on page 68, which begins, "Sir, we narrow-minded people" and the following paragraph, "Sir, I do not desire" with sufficient care to get the thought completely. Then reproduce these paragraphs, explaining fully Webster's attitude and the allusions he makes. In similar manner treat the third paragraph on page 99, beginning "This leads us," and other paragraphs that seem of marked importance.

Was the subject of the public lands the really important issue in Webster's speech? If not, what was the vital matter of controversy? Does the orator, in general, keep closely to his subject? Has Webster a well-developed sense of humor? How does the spirit shown by him compare with that of his opponents? How far do Webster's earnest personal conviction and enthusiasm make themselves felt?

Style

Simplicity, vigor and directness characterize the Gettysburg address. Do you find the same qualities in the *Reply to Hayne*? If not, how does the oratory of Lincoln differ from that of Webster? What would you say are the distinguishing characteristics of Webster's style? Do you think that it is peculiarly adapted to his subject? In your opinion, is the critic justified who says that "Seldom, in the world of letters, do we find such another heaven-scaling crag, with its feet in the deep sea, as Webster"?

Part Six

Orations
(Continued)

HOUSE OF PARLAMENT

4

Edmund Burke

Edmund Burke

1729–1797

The time when America was waging her war for independence was a stirring time in the history of the world. Great Britain had through her officials devastated India, Ireland was in a state of upheaval, and the French were on the eve of their bloodiest revolution. It was a time when the world needed great men and a time when the stimulus of events was certain to produce greatness in men. Edmund Burke was one of the leaders of the time, a man as fearless as he was eloquent in debate, and as wise and far-sighted in his policy as he was startling and effective in his defense of it. The colonies had no wiser nor more faithful friend and no friend who was more earnestly their champion. From the time when Burke made his first ringing speech on the Stamp Act till the last days of his life he was consistently the advocate of justice and freedom.

He was born in Dublin, and was one of the fifteen children of an Irish lawyer who desired this son to follow the same profession. Accordingly he was carefully educated in preparation for college and finally graduated from Trinity, Dublin, in 1748. Here he distinguished himself in no special way except for his erratic and somewhat tempestuous nature and for the enthusiasm with which he read,—absorbed at one time in one study and then entering with equal ardor in some other branch, but never permanently excellent in anything unless it was in Latin.

Upon graduation he was sent by his father to London to study law but at the end of four years Edmund, then about twenty-five years of age, abandoned the profession and resolved to devote himself to literature. This act so exasperated his father that he withdrew his support and the young man was left dependent entirely upon his own resources. The keenness of his intellect and the brilliancy of his powers of expression should have made him famous and wealthy but he was never successful in the conduct of his own affairs. While his prominence brought him a good income his extravagance and poor management left him heavily in debt in spite of the fact that admiring friends came frequently to his rescue, advancing large sums of money and cancelling heavy obligations to themselves. He purchased a large estate hoping to found an enduring house but the death of his son destroyed his hope of the peerage and the increasing burden of his debts finally drove him from public life. For the three years preceding his death he devoted himself faithfully to literary labors in the vain hope of retrieving his fallen fortunes. Lord Buckingham in his will finally freed Burke's estate and ordered the destruction of all evidences of the latter's indebtedness.

Burke was for several years an assistant to the secretary for Ireland but it was as member of parliament from Wendover that he achieved his greatest forensic triumphs. Morley says: "Burke is entitled to our lasting reverence as the first apostle and great upholder of integrity, mercy, and honor in the relation between his countrymen and their humble dependents." And it is in this capacity that we see him acting. His activity and powerful speech in the impeachment trial of Warren Hastings, February, 1788, carried Great Britain by storm. India and her wrongs were made the subject of the most soul-stirring appeals, and the ruthless tyranny by which she had been crushed was exposed with so furious a zeal and such impassioned invective that the listening multitude, spectators, advocates, judges, and even the great criminal himself, were spellbound in anxiety and terror. It was the greatest triumph of classic oratory known to modern times. Burke failed to secure the conviction of Hastings but he obtained justice for India and established mercy and moderation for the colonists.

He was a man of wonderful resources and deep learning. "I have learned more from him," said Fox, "than from all the books I ever read." "Take up whatever topic you please he is ready to meet you," was Dr. Johnson's testimony to his wide culture.

To the electors of Bristol he once gave this

manly account of his action in Parliament. Objections had been made to his conduct and after meeting and answering them he continued: "I do not stand before you accused of venality or neglect of duty. It is not said that in the long period of my service I have in a single instance sacrificed the slightest of interests to my ambition or to my future. It is not alleged that to gratify any anger or revenge of my own or of my party I have had a share in wronging or oppressing any description of men. No! The charges against me are all of one kind: that I have pushed the principles of general justice and benevolence too far — further than a cautious policy would warrant and further than the opinions of many would go along with me. In every accident which may happen through life, in pain, in sorrow, in depression and distress I will call to mind this accusation and be comforted."

I think it was on going home from the club one night that Edmund Burke, his soul full of great thoughts, be sure, for they never left him, his heart full of gentleness, was accosted by a poor, wandering woman to whom he spoke words of kindness; and, moved by her tears, perhaps having caused them by his own words, he took her home to the house of his wife and children, and never left her until he had found the means of restoring her to honesty and labor. O you fine gentlemen, you Marches and Selwyns and Chesterfields, how small you look by the side of this great man!

— Thackeray.

Burke will always be read with delight and edification, because in the midst of discussions on the local and the accidental, he scatters apothegms that take us into the regions of lasting wisdom. In the midst of the torrent of his most strenuous and passionate deliverances, he suddenly rises aloof from his immediate subject, and in all tranquillity reminds us of some permanent relation of things, some enduring truth of human life or society. We do not hear the organ tones of Milton, for faith and freedom had other notes in the seventeenth century. There is none of the complacent and wise-browed sagacity of Bacon, for Burke's were days of eager personal strife and party fire and civil division. We are not exhilarated by the cheerfulness, the polish, the fine manners of Bolingbroke, for Burke had an anxious conscience and was earnest and intent that the good should triumph. And yet Burke is among the greatest of those who have wrought marvels in the prose of our English tongue.

— Morley.

Unlike Hume, whose politics were elaborated in the study, Burke wrote his political tracts and speeches face to face with events, and upon them.

Philosophical reasoning and poetic passion were wedded together in them on the side of conservatism, and every art of eloquence was used with the mastery that imagination gives.—*Rev. Stopford Brooke.*

There are two of Burke's speeches that are intimately related — the one on *American Taxation* and the one *On Conciliation with America.* Add to these the *Letter to the Sheriffs of Bristol,* and to quote Mr. John Morley, "It is no exaggeration to say that they compose the most perfect manual in our literature, or in any literature, for one who approaches the study of public affairs, whether for knowledge or for practice. They are an example without fault of all the qualities which the critic, whether a theorist or an actor, of great political situations should strive by night and by day to possess. . . . If ever, in the fullness of time,—and surely the fates of men and literature cannot have it otherwise,— Burke becomes one of the half-dozen names of established and universal currency in education and in common books, rising above the waywardness of literary caprice or intellectual fashions, as Shakespeare and Milton and Bacon rise above it, it will be the mastery, the elevation, the wisdom of these far-shining discourses, in which the world will, in an especial degree, recognize the combination of sovereign gifts with benificent uses."

The importance of the occasion and the far-reaching consequences of the debates in which the two speeches had their origin cannot be over-estimated. The writer quoted above says in another place, "The defeat and subjugation of the colonists would have been followed by the final annihilation of the Opposition in the mother country. The War of Independence was virtually a second English Civil War. The ruin of the American cause would have been also the ruin of the constitutional cause in England; and a patriotic Englishman may revere the memory of Patrick Henry and George Washington as justly as the patriotic American. Burke's attitude in this great contest is that part of his history about the majestic and noble wisdom of which there can be least dispute."

If the great orator did not succeed in averting the war, if a headstrong and violent ministry had so far forced their oppressive measures upon the colonists as to make war inevitable, yet the eloquence of Burke and his noble allies made the war unpopular with great numbers of the loyal people of Great Britain, paved the way for the final success of American arms, and made possible the ultimate conciliation of the independent nation with Great Britain.

In the first speech Burke endeavored to bring the policy of the government back to its original method of dealing with the colonies, that of leaving them free and independent in the control of their local affairs and merely regulating their commerce. He spoke from the English standpoint and criticised vehemently the vacillating and foolish policy of the ministry. The speech was keen and sarcastic and its prime purpose was to overthrow Lord North and his cabinet. This speech was delivered in 1774.

A little less than a year later, on the twenty-second of March, 1775, the second speech was made. Here his attitude was entirely different. No longer attacking the ministry, he attempted, by showing the condition and future possibilities of the American colonies, to placate their enemies and secure for them such substantial justice as would please and satisfy them and at the same time bring valuable and willing friends to the support of the mother country. Professor Goodrich, of Yale, considers it "the most finished of Burke's speeches," and Fox, twenty years after the speech was delivered, gave it this encomium:

"Let gentlemen read this speech by day, and meditate on it by night; let them peruse it again and again, study it, imprint it on their minds, impress it on their hearts; they will then learn that *representation* is the sovereign remedy for every evil."

"Yet Erskine, who was in the House when this was delivered, said that it drove everybody away, including people who, when they came to read it, read it over and over again, and could hardly think of anything else. Burke's gestures were clumsy; he had sonorous but harsh tones; he never lost a strong Irish accent; and his utterance was often hurried and eager. Apart from these disadvantages of accident, which have been overcome by men infinitely inferior to Burke, it is easy to perceive, from the matter and texture of the speeches that have become English classics, that the very qualities which are excellencies in literature were drawbacks to the spoken discourses."

—Morley.

George III became king in 1760. By nature he was obstinate and self-willed and throughout his boyhood and early life he listened to the teachings of his mother, whose one idea was to establish an absolute monarchy, with him as its ruler. These teachings produced their natural effect and no sooner had George ascended the throne, than he began a struggle with Parliament, in which his persistent and unscrupulous character enabled him to win.

The first step in the king's policy was to form for himself a supporting party among the Tory nobles, who had been the followers of the Stuarts. He took advantage also of the dissensions which were dividing the Whig party, many of whom had been under the leadership of Walpole, favoring peace abroad and at home, and others of the younger branch wishing to assist in the continental struggles which were then under way. The history of the years immediately preceding the American Revolution, is the history of the struggle between the king, these factions among the ruling classes, and the growing discontent among the English people, who for almost the first time in their history, looked with contempt upon Parliament. And for this contempt there was good reason. Never was there a more corrupt group of men than those who formed the House of Commons. They obtained their seats by purchase and sold their votes to the highest bidder. This was usually the king. He purchased the votes not only of the members of Parliament, but sent his agents into the country and actually bought the election of his favorites in the different boroughs. By these means he obtained a control which was almost absolute and when Lord North was chosen Prime Minister he was but a cloak for George III who formulated his policy and directed his actions. All this had not taken place without the notice of the great body of the English people, whose outraged dignity found vent in constant turmoil and opposition. In some localities members were repeatedly returned against the wishes of the king, but they were so few in number that their votes counted as nothing, against those owned by the king.

It was at this time that public journalism came first to be an important factor in English politics.

The proceedings of Parliament had not been published previously, but after violent opposition extending over several years, the recently established newspapers, aided by the growing public sentiment, succeeded in obtaining full reports of the proceedings. This opened the way for that publicity which eventually brought the House of Commons back to its original position as the direct representative of the people and cleansed it from its taint of bribery. But when Burke spoke the power of the king was at its height and it was inevitable that the plan for conciliation should fail.

The condition of things in the colonies is familiar to us. The repeal of the Stamp Act might have proved a pacificatory measure, had not its significance been entirely destroyed by a declaration that Great Britain still had a right to tax the colonies. In 1767, a new tax levied caused so much agitation that Parliament decided to remove all impositions except that upon tea, this being retained in order to reserve the right. The colonists received this law in derision; in Boston the tea was thrown into the harbor by patriots disguised as Indians and elsewhere it was not permitted to land or was stored in damp cellars and left to rot in disuse.

This roused the animosity of the king and at his instigation a bill was passed closing the port of Boston, and General Gage was sent to Massachusetts to enforce submission. In addition to this a law was passed requiring all persons under indictment for criminal offenses to be sent to England for trial, the quartering of troops on citizens of Boston was authorized, and laws were passed tending to restrict the extension of colonial territory.

Meanwhile the colonies were far from idle. Oppression had brought unity of feeling among them and in September, 1774, a general congress convened at Philadelphia. War seemed certain and the colonists prepared to meet the movements of the troops sent against them. Franklin, who had been in England for some time as ambassador, recognized the impossibility of accomplishing anything and sailed for America on the very day that Burke made his plea for peace. War was on and in less than a month British soldiers had fallen at Concord Bridge.

On Conciliation with America

EDMUND BURKE

On Conciliation witb America

I HOPE, Sir, that notwithstanding the austerity of the Chair; your good nature will incline you to some degree of indulgence towards human frailty. You will not think it unnatural that those who have an object depending, which strongly engages their hopes and fears, should be somewhat inclined to superstition. As I came into the House full of anxiety about the event of my motion, I found, to my infinite surprise, that the grand penal bill, by which we had passed sentence on the trade and sustenance of America, is to be returned to us from the other House.[1] I do confess I could not help looking on this event as a fortunate omen. I look upon it as a sort of providential favor, by which we are put once more in possession of our deliberative capacity upon a business so very questionable in its nature, so very uncertain in its issue. By the

---

1. This was the bill which proposed to restrict the commerce of the colonies and to prohibit fishing on the banks of Newfoundland under certain conditions. Its enforcement would mean beggary to thousands.

return of this bill, which seemed to have taken its flight forever, we are at this very instant nearly as free to choose a plan for our American Government as we were on the first day of the session. If, Sir, we incline to the side of conciliation, we are not at all embarrassed (unless we please to make ourselves so) by any incongruous mixture of coercion and restraint. We are therefore called upon, as it were by a superior warning voice, again to attend to America; to attend to the whole of it together; and to review the subject with an unusual degree of care and calmness.

Surely it is an awful subject, or there is none so on this side of the grave. When I first had the honor of a seat in this House, the affairs of that continent pressed themselves upon us as the most important and most delicate object of Parliamentary attention. My little share in this great deliberation oppressed me.[2] I found myself a partaker in a very high trust; and, having no sort of reason to rely on the strength of my natural abilities for the proper execution of that trust, I was obliged to take more than common pains to instruct myself in everything which relates to our

---

2. In 1765, Burke represented Wendover, and his maiden speech was for the repeal of the Stamp Act.

Colonies. I was not less under the necessity of forming some fixed ideas concerning the general policy of the British Empire. Something of this sort seemed to be indispensable, in order, amidst so vast a fluctuation of passions and opinions, to concenter my thoughts, to ballast my conduct, to preserve me from being blown about by every wind of fashionable doctrine. I really did not think it safe or manly to have fresh principles to seek upon every fresh mail which should arrive from America.

At that period I had the fortune to find myself in perfect concurrence with a large majority in this House.[3] Bowing under that high authority, and penetrated with the sharpness and strength of that early impression, I have continued ever since, without the least deviation, in my original sentiments. Whether this be owing to an obstinate perseverance in error, or to a religious adherence to what appears to me truth and reason, it is in your equity to judge.

Sir, Parliament, having an enlarged view of objects, made, during this interval,[4] more frequent changes in their sentiments and their

---

3. The repeal of the Stamp Act.
4. December, 1765, to March, 1775.

conduct than could be justified in a particular person upon the contracted scale of private information. But though I do not hazard anything approaching to a censure on the motives of former Parliaments to all those alterations, one fact is undoubted — that under them the state of America has been kept in continual agitation. Everything administered as remedy to the public complaint, if it did not produce, was at least followed by, an heightening of the distemper; until, by a variety of experiments, that important country has been brought into her present situation — a situation I will not miscall, which I dare not name, which I scarcely know how to comprehend in the terms of any description.

In this posture, Sir, things stood at the beginning of the session. About that time, a worthy member of great Parliamentary experience,[5] who, in the year 1766, filled the chair of the American committee with much ability, took me aside; and, lamenting the present aspect of our politics, told me things were come to such a pass that our former methods of proceeding in the House would be no longer tolerated: that the public tribunal (never too indulgent to a long and unsuccess-

5. Mr. Rose Fuller.

ful opposition) would now scrutinize our conduct with unusual severity: that the very vicissitudes and shiftings of ministerial measures, instead of convicting their authors of inconstancy and want of system, would be taken as an occasion of charging us with a predetermined discontent, which nothing could satisfy; whilst we accused every measure of vigor as cruel, and every proposal of lenity as weak and irresolute. The public, he said, would not have patience to see us play the game out with our adversaries; we must produce our hand. It would be expected that those who for many years had been active in such affairs should show that they had formed some clear and decided idea of the principles of Colony government; and were capable of drawing out something like a platform of the ground which might be laid for future and permanent tranquillity.

I felt the truth of what my honorable friend represented; but I felt my situation too. His application might have been made with far greater propriety to many other gentlemen. No man was indeed ever better disposed, or worse qualified, for such an undertaking than myself. Though I gave so far in to his opinion that I immediately threw my thoughts into a sort of Parliamentary form, I was by no means equally ready to produce them. It generally argues some degree of natural impotence of mind, or some want of knowledge of the world, to hazard plans of government except from a seat of authority. Propositions are made, not only ineffectually, but somewhat disreputably, when the minds of men are not properly disposed for their reception; and, for my part, I am not ambitious of ridicule — not absolutely a candidate for disgrace.

Besides, Sir, to speak the plain truth, I have in general no very exalted opinion of the virtue of paper government; nor of any politics in which the plan is to be wholly separated from the execution. But when I saw that anger and violence prevailed every day more and more, and that things were hastening towards an incurable alienation of our Colonies, I confess my caution gave way. I felt this as one of those few moments in which decorum yields to a higher duty. Public calamity is a mighty leveler; and there are occasions when any, even the slightest, chance of doing good must be laid hold on, even by the most inconsiderable person.

To restore order and repose to an empire so great and so distracted as ours, is, merely in the attempt, an undertaking that would ennoble the flights of the highest genius, and obtain pardon for the efforts of the meanest understanding. Struggling a good while with these thoughts, by degrees I felt myself more firm. I derived, at length, some confidence from what in other circumstances usually produces timidity. I grew less anxious, even from the idea of my own insignificance. For, judging of what you are by what you ought to be, I persuaded myself that you would not reject a reasonable proposition because it had nothing but its reason to recommend it. On the other hand, being totally destitute of all shadow of influence, natural or adventitious, I was very sure that, if my proposition were futile or dangerous — if it were weakly conceived, or improperly timed — there was nothing exterior to it of power to awe, dazzle, or delude you. You will see it just as it is; and you will treat it just as it deserves.

The proposition is peace. Not peace through the medium of war; not peace to be hunted through the labyrinth of intricate and endless negotiations; not peace to arise out of universal discord fomented, from principle, in all parts of the Empire; not peace to depend on the juridical determination of perplexing questions, or the precise marking the shadowy boundaries of a complex government. It is simple peace; sought in its natural course, and in its ordinary haunts. It is peace sought in the spirit of peace, and laid in principles purely specific. I propose, by removing the ground of the difference, and by restoring the former unsuspecting confidence of the Colonies in the Mother Country, to give permanent satisfaction to your people; and (far from a scheme of ruling by discord) to reconcile them to each other in the same act and by the bond of the very same interest which reconciles them to British government.

My idea is nothing more. Refined policy ever has been the parent of confusion; and ever will be so, as long as the world endures. Plain good intention, which is as easily discovered at the first view as fraud is surely detected at last, is, let me say, of no mean force in the government of mankind. Genuine simplicity of heart is an healing and cementing principle. My plan, therefore, being formed upon the most simple grounds imaginable, may disappoint some people when they hear it. It has nothing to recommend it to the pruriency of curious ears. There is nothing at all new and captivating in it. It has nothing of the splendor of the project which has been lately laid upon your table by the noble lord in the blue ribbon.[6] It does not propose to fill your lobby with squabbling Colony agents, who will require the interposition of your mace, at every instant, to keep the peace amongst them. It does not institute a magnificent auction of finance, where captivated provinces come to general ransom by bidding against each other, until you knock down the hammer, and determine a proportion of payment beyond all the powers of algebra to equalize and settle.

The plan which I shall presume to suggest derives, however, one great advantage from the proposition and registry of that noble lord's project. The idea of conciliation is admissible. First, the House, in accepting the resolution moved by the noble lord, has admitted, notwithstanding the menacing front of our address,[7] notwithstanding our heavy bills of pains and penalties — that we do not think ourselves precluded from all ideas of free grace and bounty.

6. Lord North, the Prime Minister, wore the badge of a Knight of the Garter. His measure passed February 27, 1775, was the one which agreed to forbear to tax any Colony which should propose to contribute its proportion to the common defense.

7. An address to the king which declared that Massachusetts was in rebellion urged his majesty to act at once.

The House has gone farther; it has declared conciliation admissible, previous to any submission on the part of America. It has even shot a good deal beyond that mark, and has admitted that the complaints of our former mode of exerting the right of taxation were not wholly unfounded. That right thus exerted is allowed to have something reprehensible in it, something unwise, or something grievous; since, in the midst of our heat and resentment, we, of ourselves, have proposed a capital alteration; and in order to get rid of what seemed so very exceptionable, have instituted a mode that is altogether new; one that is, indeed, wholly alien from all the ancient methods and forms of Parliament.

The principle of this proceeding is large enough for my purpose. The means proposed by the noble lord for carrying his ideas into execution, I think, indeed, are very indifferently suited to the end; and this I shall endeavor to show you before I sit down. But, for the present, I take my ground on the admitted principle. I mean to give peace. Peace implies reconciliation; and where there has been a material dispute, reconciliation does in a manner always imply concession on the one part or on the other. In this state of things I make no difficulty in affirming that the proposal ought to originate from us. Great and acknowledged force is not impaired, either in effect or in opinion, by an unwillingness to exert itself. The superior power may offer peace with honor and with safety. Such an offer from such a power will be attributed to magnanimity. But the concessions of the weak are the concessions of fear. When such a one is disarmed, he is wholly at the mercy of his superior; and he loses forever that time and those chances, which, as they happen to all men, are the strength and resources of all inferior power.

The capital leading questions on which you must this day decide are these two: First, whether you ought to concede; and secondly, what your concession ought to be. On the first of these questions we have gained, as I have just taken the liberty of observing to you, some ground. But I am sensible that a good deal more is still to be done. Indeed, Sir, to enable us to determine both on the one and the other of these great questions with a firm and precise judgment, I think it may be necessary to consider distinctly the true nature and the peculiar circumstances of the object which we have before us; because after all our struggle, whether we will or not, we must govern America according to that nature and to those circumstances, and not according to our own imaginations, nor according to abstract ideas of right — by no means according to mere general theories of government, the resort to which appears to me, in our present situation, no better than arrant trifling. I shall therefore endeavor, with your leave, to lay before you some of the most material of these circumstances in as full and as clear a manner as I am able to state them.

The first thing that we have to consider with regard to the nature of the object is — the number of people in the Colonies. I have taken for some years a good deal of pains on that point. I can by no calculation justify myself in placing the number below two millions of inhabitants of our own European blood and color, besides at least five hundred thousand others, who form no inconsiderable part of the strength and opulence of the whole. This, Sir, is, I believe, about the true number. There is no occasion to exaggerate where plain truth is of so much weight and importance. But whether I put the present numbers too high or too low is a matter of little moment. Such is the strength with which population shoots in that part of the world, that, state the numbers as high as we will, whilst the dispute continues, the exaggeration ends. Whilst we are discussing any given magnitude, they are grown to it. Whilst we spend our time in deliberating on the mode of governing two millions, we shall find we have millions more to manage. Your children do not grow faster from infancy to manhood than they spread from families to communities, and from villages to nations.

I put this consideration of the present and the growing numbers in the front of our deliberation, because, Sir, this consideration will make it evident to a blunter discernment than yours, that no partial, narrow, contracted, pinched, occasional system will be at all suitable to such an object. It will show you that it is not to be considered as one of those *minima*[8] which are out of the eye and consideration of the law; not a paltry excrescence of the state; not a mean dependent, who may be neglected with little damage and provoked with little danger. It will prove that some degree of care and caution is required in the handling of such an object; it will show that you

---

8. *Minima — little things.* It is a maxim that the law does not concern itself with little things.

ought not, in reason, to trifle with so large a mass of the interests and feelings of the human race. You could at no time do so without guilt; and be assured you will not be able to do it long with impunity.

But the population of this country, the great and growing population, though a very important consideration, will lose much of its weight if not combined with other circumstances. The commerce of your Colonies is out of all proportion beyond the numbers of the people. This ground of their commerce indeed has been trod some days ago, and with great ability, by a distinguished person at your bar.[9] This gentleman, after thirty-five years — it is so long since he first appeared at the same place to plead for the commerce of Great Britain — has come again before you to plead the same cause, without any other effect of time, than that to the fire of imagination and extent of erudition which even then marked him as one of the first literary characters of his age, he has added a consummate knowledge in the commercial interest of his country, formed by a long course of enlightened and discriminating experience.

---

9. Mr. Glover presented a petition from West Indian planters, asking for peace as their commerce was suffering.

Sir, I should be inexcusable in coming after such a person with any detail, if a great part of the members who now fill the House had not the misfortune to be absent when he appeared at your bar. Besides, Sir, I propose to take the matter at periods of time somewhat different from his. There is, if I mistake not, a point of view from whence, if you will look at the subject, it is impossible that it should not make an impression upon you.

[The speaker here presents statistics showing how the commerce of the Colonists has grown and in what lines. His summing up follows.]

The trade with America alone is now within less than £500,000 of being equal to what this great commercial nation, England, carried on at the beginning of this century with the whole world! If I had taken the largest year of those on your table, it would rather have exceeded. But, it will be said, is not this American trade an unnatural protuberance, that has drawn the juices from the rest of the body? The reverse. It is the very food that has nourished every other part into its present magnitude. Our general trade has been greatly augmented, and augmented more or less in almost every part to which it ever extended;

but with this material difference, that of the six millions which in the beginning of the century constituted the whole mass of our export commerce, the Colony trade was but one-twelfth part; it is now (as a part of sixteen millions) considerably more than a third of the whole. This is the relative proportion of the importance of the Colonies at these two periods; and all reasoning concerning our mode of treating them must have this proportion as its basis; or it is a reasoning weak, rotten, and sophistical.

Mr. Speaker, I cannot prevail on myself to hurry over this great consideration. *It is good for us to be here.* We stand where we have an immense view of what is, and what is past. Clouds, indeed, and darkness, rest upon the future. Let us, however, before we descend from this noble eminence, reflect that this growth of our national prosperity has happened within the short period of the life of man. It has happened within sixty-eight years. There are those alive whose memory might touch the two extremities. For instance, my Lord Bathurst[10] might remember all the stages of the progress. He was in 1704 of an age at

---

10. Then about ninety-one years of age.

ւeast to be made to comprehend such things. He was then old enough *acta parentum jam legere, et quæ sit potuit cognoscere virtus.*[11] Suppose, Sir, that the angel of this auspicious youth, foreseeing the many virtues which make him one of the most amiable, as he is one of the most fortunate, men of his age, had opened to him in vision that when, in the fourth generation, the third Prince of the House of Brunswick had sat twelve years on the throne of that nation which, by the happy issue of moderate and healing counsels, was to be made Great Britain, he should see his son, Lord Chancellor of England, turn back the current of hereditary dignity to its fountain, and raise him to a higher rank of peerage, whilst he enriched the family with a new one — if, amidst these bright and happy scenes of domestic honor and prosperity, that angel should have drawn up the curtain, and unfolded the rising glories of his country, and, whilst he was gazing with admiration on the then commercial grandeur of England, the genius should point out to him a little speck, scarcely visible in the mass of the national interest, a small seminal principle, rather than

---

11. Now he was able to understand the deeds of his parents and to know what virtue is.—*Virgil.*

a formed body, and should tell him: "Young man, there is America — which at this day serves for little more than to amuse you with stories of savage men, and uncouth manners; yet shall, before you taste of death, show itself equal to the whole of that commerce which now attracts the envy of the world. Whatever England has been growing to by a progressive increase of improvement, brought in by varieties of people, by succession of civilizing conquests and civilizing settlements in a series of seventeen hundred years, you shall see as much added to her by America in the course of a single life!" If this state of his country had been foretold to him, would it not require all the sanguine credulity of youth, and all the fervid glow of enthusiasm, to make him believe it? Fortunate man, he has lived to see it! Fortunate, indeed, if he lives to see nothing that shall vary the prospect, and cloud the setting of his day!

Excuse me, Sir, if turning from such thoughts I resume this comparative view once more. You have seen it on a large scale; look at it on a small one. I will point out to your attention a particular instance of it in the single province of Pennsylvania. In the year 1704 that province called for £11,459 in value of your commodities, native and foreign. This was the whole. What did it demand in 1772? Why, nearly fifty times as much; for in that year the export to Pennsylvania was £507,909, nearly equal to the export to all the Colonies together in the first period.

I choose, Sir, to enter into these minute and particular details, because generalities, which in all other cases are apt to heighten and raise the subject, have here a tendency to sink it. When we speak of the commerce with our Colonies, fiction lags after truth, invention is unfruitful, and imagination cold and barren.

So far, Sir, as to the importance of the object, in view of its commerce, as concerned in the exports from England. If I were to detail the imports, I could show how many enjoyments they procure which deceive the burthen of life; how many materials which invigorate the springs of national industry, and extend and animate every part of our foreign and domestic commerce. This would be a curious subject indeed; but I must prescribe bounds to myself in a matter so vast and various.

I pass, therefore, to the Colonies in another point of view, their agriculture. This they have prosecuted with such a spirit, that, besides feeding plentifully their own growing multitude, their annual export of grain, comprehending rice, has some years ago exceeded a million in value. Of their last harvest I am persuaded they will export much more. At the beginning of the century some of these Colonies imported corn from the Mother Country. For some time past the Old World has been fed from the New. The scarcity which you have felt would have been a desolating famine, if this child of your old age, with a true filial piety, with a Roman charity, had not put the full breast of its youthful exuberance to the mouth of its exhausted parent. [12]

As to the wealth which the Colonies have drawn from the sea by their fisheries, you had all that matter fully opened at your bar. You surely thought those acquisitions of value, for they seemed even to excite your envy; and yet the spirit by which that enterprising employment has been exercised ought rather, in my opinion, to have raised your esteem and admiration. And pray, Sir, what in the world is equal to it ? Pass by the other parts, and look at the manner in which the people of

---

12. There is a Roman legend of a daughter nourishing from her own breasts her aged father imprisoned in his cell.

New England have of late carried on the whale fishery. Whilst we follow them among the tumbling mountains of ice, and behold them penetrating into the deepest frozen recesses of Hudson's Bay and Davis's Straits, whilst we are looking for them beneath the Arctic circle, we hear that they have pierced into the opposite region of polar cold, that they are at the antipodes, and engaged under the frozen Serpent of the south.[13] Falkland Island, which seemed too remote and romantic an object for the grasp of national ambition, is but a stage and resting-place in the progress of their victorious industry. Nor is the equinoctial heat more discouraging to them than the accumulated winter of both the poles. We know that whilst some of them draw the line and strike the harpoon on the coast of Africa, others run the longitude and pursue their gigantic game along the coast of Brazil. No sea but what is vexed by their fisheries; no climate that is not witness to their toils. Neither the perseverance of Holland, nor the activity of France, nor the dexterous and firm sagacity of English enterprise ever carried this most perilous mode of hardy industry to the extent to which it has been pushed by this

13. A constellation in the far southern heavens.

recent people; a people who are still, as it were, but in the gristle, and not yet hardened into the bone of manhood.

When I contemplate these things; when I know that the Colonies in general owe little or nothing to any care of ours, and that they are not squeezed into this happy form by the constraints of watchful and suspicious government, but that, through a wise and salutary neglect, a generous nature has been suffered to take her own way to perfection; when I reflect upon these effects, when I see how profitable they have been to us, I feel all the pride of power sink, and all presumption in the wisdom of human contrivances melt and die away within me. My rigor relents. I pardon something to the spirit of liberty.

I am sensible, Sir, that all which I have asserted in my detail is admitted in the gross; but that quite a different conclusion is drawn from it. America, gentlemen say, is a noble object. It is an object well worth fighting for. Certainly it is, if fighting a people be the best way of gaining them. Gentlemen in this respect will be led to their choice of means by their complexions and their habits. Those who understand the military art will of course have some predilection for it. Those who wield the thunder of the state may have more confidence in the efficacy of arms. But I confess, possibly for want of this knowledge, my opinion is much more in favor of prudent management than of force; considering force not as an odious, but a feeble, instrument for preserving a people so numerous, so active, so growing, so spirited as this, in a profitable and subordinate connection with us.

First, Sir, permit me to observe that the use of force alone is but temporary. It may subdue for a moment, but it does not remove the necessity of subduing again; and a nation is not governed which is perpetually to be conquered.

My next objection is its uncertainty. Terror is not always the effect of force, and an armament is not a victory. If you do not succeed, you are without resource; for, conciliation failing, force remains; but, force failing, no further hope of reconciliation is left. Power and authority are sometimes bought by kindness; but they can never be begged as alms by an impoverished and defeated violence.

A further objection to force is, that you impair the object by your very endeavors to preserve it. The thing you fought for is not the thing which you recover; but depreciated, sunk,

wasted, and consumed in the contest. Nothing less will content me than *whole America.*
I do not choose to consume its strength along
with our own, because in all parts it is the British strength that I consume. I do not choose to
be caught by a foreign enemy at the end of
this exhausting conflict; and still less in the
midst of it. I may escape; but I can make no
insurance against such an event. Let me
add, that I do not choose wholly to break the
American spirit; because it is the spirit that
has made the country.

Lastly, we have no sort of experience in
favor of force as an instrument in the rule of
our Colonies. Their growth and their utility
have been owing to methods altogether different. Our ancient indulgence has been said
to be pursued to a fault. It may be so. But
we know, if feeling is evidence, that our fault
was more tolerable than our attempt to mend
it ; and our sin far more salutary than our
penitence.

These, Sir, are my reasons for not entertaining that high opinion of untried force by
which many gentlemen, for whose sentiments
in other particulars I have great respect, seem
to be so greatly captivated. But there is still
behind a third consideration concerning this

object which serves to determine my opinion on the sort of policy which ought to be pursued in the management of America, even more than its population and its commerce— I mean its temper and character.

In this character of the Americans, a love of freedom is the predominating feature which marks and distinguishes the whole; and as an ardent is always a jealous affection, your Colonies become suspicious, restive, and untractable whenever they see the least attempt to wrest from them by force, or shuffle from them by chicane, what they think the only advantage worth living for. This fierce spirit of liberty is stronger in the English Colonies probably than in any other people of the earth, and this from a great variety of powerful causes; which, to understand the true temper of their minds and the direction which this spirit ·takes, it will not be amiss to lay open somewhat more largely.

First, the people of the Colonies are descendants of Englishmen. England, Sir, is a nation which still, I hope, respects, and formerly adored, her freedom. The Colonists emigrated from you when this part of your character was most predominant; and they took this bias and direction the moment they

parted from your hands. They are therefore
not only devoted to liberty, but to liberty
according to English ideas, and on English
principles. Abstract liberty, like other mere
abstractions, is not to be found. Liberty
inheres in some sensible object; and every
nation has formed to itself some favorite
point, which by way of eminence becomes the
criterion of their happiness. It happened, you
know, Sir, that the great contests for freedom
in this country were from the earliest times
chiefly upon the question of taxing. Most of
the contests in the ancient commonwealths
turned primarily on the right of election of
magistrates; or on the balance among the
several orders of the state. The question of
money was not with them so immediate. But
in England it was otherwise. On this point
of taxes the ablest pens, and most eloquent
tongues, have been exercised; the greatest
spirits have acted and suffered.

In order to give the fullest satisfaction concerning the importance of this point, it was
not only necessary for those who in argument
defended the excellence of the English Constitution to insist on this privilege of granting
money as a dry point of fact, and to prove
that the right had been acknowledged in

ancient parchments and blind usages to reside in a certain body called a House of Commons. They went much farther; they attempted to prove, and they succeeded, that in theory it ought to be so, from the particular nature of a House of Commons as an immediate representative of the people, whether the old records had delivered this oracle or not. They took infinite pains to inculcate, as a fundamental principle, that in all monarchies the people must in effect themselves, mediately or immediately, possess the power of granting their own money, or no shadow of liberty can subsist. The Colonies draw from you, as with their life-blood, these ideas and principles. Their love of liberty, as with you, fixed and attached on this specific point of taxing. Liberty might be safe, or might be endangered, in twenty other particulars, without their being much pleased or alarmed. Here they felt its pulse; and as they found that beat, they thought themselves sick or sound. I do not say whether they were right or wrong in applying your general arguments to their own case. It is not easy, indeed, to make a monopoly of theorems and corollaries. The fact is, that they did thus apply those general arguments; and your mode of governing them, whether through lenity or indolence, through wisdom or mistake, confirmed them in the imagination that they, as well as you, had an interest in these common principles.

They were further confirmed in this pleasing error by the form of their provincial legislative assemblies. Their governments are popular in an high degree; some are merely popular; in all, the popular representative is the most weighty; and this share of the people in their ordinary government never fails to inspire them with lofty sentiments, and with a strong aversion from whatever tends to deprive them of their chief importance.

If anything were wanting to this necessary operation of the form of government, religion would have given it a complete effect. Religion, always a principle of energy, in this new people is no way worn out or impaired; and their mode of professing it is also one main cause of this free spirit. The people are Protestants; and of that kind which is the most adverse to all implicit submission of mind and opinion. This is a persuasion not only favorable to liberty, but built upon it. I do not think, Sir, that the reason of this averseness in the dissenting churches from all that looks like absolute government is so much to be sought in their religious tenets, as in their history.

Every one knows that the Roman Catholic religion is at least coëval with most of the governments where it prevails; that it has generally gone hand in hand with them, and received great favor and every kind of support from authority. The Church of England too was formed from her cradle under the nursing care of regular government. But the dissenting interests have sprung up in direct opposition to all the ordinary powers of the world, and could justify that opposition only on a strong claim to natural liberty. Their very existence depended on the powerful and unremitted assertion of that claim. All Protestantism, even the most cold and passive, is a sort of dissent.

But the religion most prevalent in our Northern Colonies is a refinement on the principle of resistance; it is the dissidence of dissent, and the protestantism of the Protestant religion. This religion, under a variety of denominations agreeing in nothing but in the communion of the spirit of liberty, is predominant in most of the Northern Provinces, where the Church of England, notwithstanding its legal rights, is in reality no more than a sort of private sect, not composing most probably the tenth of the people. The Colonists left England when this spirit was high, and in the emigrants was the highest of all; and even that stream of foreigners which has been constantly flowing into these Colonies has, for the greatest part, been composed of dissenters from the establishments of their several countries, who have brought with them a temper and character far from alien to that of the people with whom they mixed.

Sir, I can perceive by their manner that some gentlemen object to the latitude of this description, because in the Southern Colonies the Church of England forms a large body, and has a regular establishment. It is certainly true. There is, however, a circumstance attending these Colonies which, in my opinion, fully counterbalances this difference, and makes the spirit of liberty still more high and haughty than in those to the northward. It is that in Virginia and the Carolinas they have a vast multitude of slaves. Where this is the case in any part of the world, those who are free are by far the most proud and jealous of their freedom. Freedom is to them not only an enjoyment, but a kind of rank

INTERIOR OF THE HOUSE OF COMMONS

and privilege. Not seeing there, that freedom, as in countries where it is a common
blessing and as broad and general as the air,
may be united with much abject toil, with
great misery, with all the exterior of servitude,— liberty looks, amongst them, like
something that is more noble and liberal. I
do not mean, Sir, to commend the superior
morality of this sentiment, which has at least
as much pride as virtue in it; but I cannot
alter the nature of man. The fact is so; and
these people of the Southern Colonies are
much more strongly, and with an higher and
more stubborn spirit, attached to liberty than
those to the northward. Such were all the
ancient commonwealths; such were our Gothic
ancestors; such were the Poles; such will be
all masters of slaves, who are not slaves themselves. In such a people the haughtiness of
domination combines with the spirit of freedom, fortifies it, and renders it invincible.

Permit me, Sir, to add another circumstance
in our colonies which contributes no mean
part towards the growth and effect of this
untractable spirit. I mean their education.
In no country perhaps in the world is the law
so general a study. The profession itself is
numerous and powerful; and in most provinces

it takes the lead. The greater number of the deputies sent to the Congress were lawyers. But all who read, and most do read, endeavor to obtain some smattering in that science. I have been told by an eminent bookseller, that in no branch of his business, after tracts of popular devotion, were so many books as those on the law exported to the Plantations. The Colonists have now fallen into the way of printing them for their own use. I hear that they have sold nearly as many of Blackstone's Commentaries in America as in England.

General Gage marks out this disposition very particularly in a letter on your table. He states that all the people in his government are lawyers, or smatterers in law; and that in Boston they have been enabled, by successful chicane,[14] wholly to evade many parts of one of your capital penal constitutions. The smartness of debate will say that this knowledge ought to teach them more clearly the rights of legislature, their obligations to obedience, and the penalties of rebellion. All this is mighty well. But my honorable and learned friend on the floor,[15] who condescends to mark what I say for animad-

---

14. They held town meetings, though contrary to law.
15. The attorney general.

version, will disdain that ground. He has heard, as well as I, that when great honors and great emoluments do not win over this knowledge to the service of the state, it is a formidable adversary to government. If the spirit be not tamed and broken by these happy methods, it is stubborn and litigious. *Abeunt studia in mores.*[16] This study renders men acute, inquisitive, dexterous, prompt in attack, ready in defense, full of resources. In other countries, the people, more simple, and of a less mercurial cast, judge of an ill principle in government only by an actual grievance; here they anticipate the evil, and judge of the pressure of the grievance by the badness of the principle. They augur misgovernment at a distance, and snuff the approach of tyranny in every tainted breeze.

The last cause of this disobedient spirit in the Colonies is hardly less powerful than the rest, as it is not merely moral, but laid deep in the natural constitution of things. Three thousand miles of ocean lie between you and them. No contrivance can prevent the effect of this distance in weakening government. Seas roll, and months pass, between the order and the execution; and the want of a speedy

---

16. Character is influenced by studies.— *Ovid.*

explanation of a single point is enough to defeat a whole system. You have, indeed, winged ministers of vengeance, who carry your bolts in their pounces to the remotest verge of the sea. But there a power steps in that limits the arrogance of raging passions and furious elements, and says, *So far shalt thou go, and no farther*. Who are you, that you should fret and rage, and bite the chains of nature? Nothing worse happens to you than does to all nations who have extensive empire; and it happens in all the forms into which empire can be thrown. In large bodies the circulation of power must be less vigorous at the extremities. Nature has said it. The Turk cannot govern Egypt and Arabia and Kurdistan as he governs Thrace; nor has he the same dominion in Crimea and Algiers which he has at Brusa and Smyrna. Despotism itself is obliged to truck and huckster. The Sultan gets such obedience as he can. He governs with a loose rein, that he may govern at all; and the whole of the force and vigor of his authority in his center is derived from a prudent relaxation in all his borders. Spain, in her provinces, is, perhaps, not so well obeyed as you are in yours. She complies, too; she submits; she watches times.

This is the immutable condition, the eternal law of extensive and detached empire.

Then, Sir, from these six capital sources — of descent, of form of government, of religion in the Northern Provinces, of manners in the Southern, of education, of the remoteness of situation from the first mover of government — from all these causes a fierce spirit of liberty has grown up. It has grown with the growth of the people in your Colonies, and increased with the increase of their wealth; a spirit that unhappily meeting with an exercise of power in England which, however lawful, is not reconcilable to any ideas of liberty, much less with theirs, has kindled this flame that is ready to consume us.

I do not mean to commend either the spirit in this excess, or the moral causes which produce it. Perhaps a more smooth and accommodating spirit of freedom in them would be more acceptable to us. Perhaps ideas of liberty might be desired more reconcilable with an arbitrary and boundless authority. Perhaps we might wish the Colonists to be persuaded that their liberty is more secure when held in trust for them by us, as their guardians during a perpetual minority, than with any part of it in their own hands. The question is, not whether their spirit deserves praise or blame, but — what, in the name of God, shall we do with it? You have before you the object, such as it is, with all its glories, with all its imperfections on its head. You see the magnitude, the importance, the temper, the habits, the disorders. By all these considerations we are strongly urged to determine something concerning it. We are called upon to fix some rule and line for our future conduct which may give a little stability to our politics, and prevent the return of such unhappy deliberations as the present. Every such return will bring the matter before us in a still more untractable form. For, what astonishing and incredible things have we not seen already! What monsters have not been generated from this unnatural contention! Whilst every principle of authority and resistance has been pushed, upon both sides, as far as it would go, there is nothing so solid and certain, either in reasoning or in practice, that has not been shaken. Until very lately all authority in America seemed to be nothing but an emanation from yours. Even the popular part of the Colony Constitution derived all its activity and its first vital movement from the pleasure of the Crown. We thought, Sir, that the utmost which the discontented Colonists could do was to disturb authority; we never dreamt they could of themselves supply it — knowing in general what an operose business it is to establish a government absolutely new. But having, for our purposes in this contention, resolved that none but an obedient Assembly should sit, the humors of the people there, finding all passage through the legal channel stopped, with great violence broke out another way. Some provinces have tried their experiment, as we have tried ours; and theirs has succeeded. They have formed a government sufficient for its purposes, without the bustle of a revolution or the troublesome formality of an election. Evident necessity and tacit consent have done the business in an instant. So well they have done it, that Lord Dunmore [17] — the account is among the fragments on your table — tells you that the new institution is infinitely better obeyed than the ancient government ever was in its most fortunate periods. Obedience is what makes government, and not the names by which it is called; not the name of Governor, as formerly, or Committee, as at present. This new government has originated directly

17. One of the governors of Virginia.

from the people, and was not transmitted through any of the ordinary artificial media of a positive constitution. It was not a manufacture ready formed, and transmitted to them in that condition from England. The evil arising from hence is this: the Colonists having found the possibility of enjoying the advantages of order in the midst of a struggle for liberty, such struggles will not henceforward seem so terrible to the settled and sober part of mankind as they had appeared before.

Pursuing the same plan of punishing by the denial of the exercise of government to still greater lengths, we wholly abrogated the ancient government of Massachusetts. We were confident that the first feeling, if not the very prospect, of anarchy would instantly enforce a complete submission. The experiment was tried. A new, strange, unexpected face of things appeared. Anarchy is found tolerable. A vast province has now subsisted, and subsisted in a considerable degree of health and vigor for near a twelvemonth, without Governor, without public Council, without judges, without executive magistrates. How long it will continue in this state, or what may arise out of this unheard-of situation, how can the wisest of us conjecture?

Our late experience has taught us that many of those fundamental principles, formerly believed infallible, are either not of the importance they were imagined to be, or that we have not at all adverted to some other far more important and far more powerful principles, which entirely overrule those we had considered as omnipotent. I am much against any further experiments which tend to put to the proof any more of these allowed opinions which contribute so much to the public tranquillity. In effect, we suffer as much at home by this loosening of all ties, and this concussion of all established opinions, as we do abroad; for in order to prove that the Americans have no right to their liberties, we are every day endeavoring to subvert the maxims which preserve the whole spirit of our own. To prove that the Americans ought not to be free, we are obliged to depreciate the value of freedom itself; and we never seem to gain a paltry advantage over them in debate without attacking some of those principles, or deriding some of those feelings, for which our ancestors have shed their blood.

But, Sir, in wishing to put an end to pernicious experiments, I do not mean to preclude the fullest inquiry. Far from it. Far from deciding on a sudden or partial view, I would patiently go round and round the subject, and survey it minutely in every possible aspect. Sir, if I were capable of engaging you to an equal attention, I would state that, as far as I am capable of discerning, there are but three ways of proceeding relative to this stubborn spirit which prevails in your Colonies, and disturbs your government. These are — to change that spirit, as inconvenient, by removing the causes; to prosecute it as criminal; or to comply with it as necessary. I would not be guilty of an imperfect enumeration; I can think of but these three. Another has indeed been started,— that of giving up the Colonies; but it met so slight a reception that I do not think myself obliged to dwell a great while upon it. It is nothing but a little sally of anger, like the frowardness of peevish children, who, when they cannot get all they would have, are resolved to take nothing.

The first of these plans — to change the spirit, as inconvenient, by removing the causes — I think is the most like a systematic proceeding. It is radical in its principle; but it is attended with great difficulties, some of them little short, as I conceive, of impossibilities. This will appear by examining into the plans which have been proposed.

As the growing population in the Colonies is evidently one cause of their resistance, it was last session mentioned in both Houses, by men of weight, and received not without applause, that in order to check this evil it would be proper for the Crown to make no further grants of land. But to this scheme there are two objections. The first, that there is already so much unsettled land in private hands as to afford room for an immense future population, although the Crown not only withheld its grants, but annihilated its soil. If this be the case, then the only effect of this avarice of desolation, this hoarding of a royal wilderness, would be to raise the value of the possessions in the hands of the great private monopolists, without any adequate check to the growing and alarming mischief of population.

But if you stopped your grants, what would be the consequence? The people would occupy without grants. They have already so occupied in many places. You cannot station garrisons in every part of these deserts. If you drive the people from one place, they will carry on their annual tillage, and remove with their flocks and herds to another. Many of the people in the back settlements are already little attached to particular situations. Already

they have topped the Appalachian Mountains.
From thence they behold before them an
immense plain, one vast, rich, level meadow;
a square of five hundred miles. Over this
they would wander without a possibility of
restraint; they would change their manners
with the habits of their life; would soon forget
a government by which they were disowned;
would become hordes of English Tartars; and,
pouring down upon your unfortified frontiers a
fierce and irresistible cavalry, become masters
of your governors and your counsellors, your
collectors and comptrollers, and of all the
slaves that adhered to them. Such would,
and in no long time must be, the effect of
attempting to forbid as a crime and to suppress as an evil the command and · blessing
of providence, *Increase and multiply*. Such
would be the happy result of the endeavor to
keep as a lair of wild beasts that earth which
God, by an express charter, has given to the
children of men.

Far different, and surely much wiser, has
been our policy hitherto. Hitherto we have
invited our people, by every kind of bounty,
to fixed establishments. We have invited the
husbandman to look to authority for his title.
We have taught him piously to believe in the

mysterious virtue of wax and parchment. We have thrown each tract of land, as it was peopled, into districts, that the ruling power should never be wholly out of sight ; and we have carefully attended every settlement with government.

Adhering, Sir, as I do, to this policy, as well as for the reasons I have just given, I think this new project of hedging-in population to be neither prudent nor practicable.

To impoverish the Colonies in general, and in particular to arrest the noble course of their maritime enterprises, would be a more easy task. I freely confess it. We have shown ·a disposition to a system of this kind, a disposition even to continue the restraint after the offense, looking on ourselves as rivals to our Colonies, and persuaded that of course we must gain all that they shall lose. Much mischief we may certainly do. The power inadequate to all other things is often more than sufficient for this. I do not look on the direct and immediate power of the Colonies to resist our violence as very formidable. In this, however, I may be mistaken. But when I consider that we have Colonies for no purpose but to be serviceable to us, it seems to my poor understanding a little preposterous

to make them unserviceable in order to keep
them obedient.   It is, in truth, nothing more
than the old and, as I thought, exploded prob-
lem of tyranny, which proposes to beggar its
subjects into submission.   But remember,
when you have completed your system of
impoverishment, that nature still proceeds
in her ordinary course; that discontent will
increase with misery; and that there are criti-
cal moments in the fortune of all states when
they who are too weak to contribute to your
prosperity may be strong enough to complete
your ruin.   *Spoliatis arma supersunt.*[18]

The temper and character which prevail in
our Colonies are, I am afraid, unalterable
by any human art.   We cannot, I fear, falsify
the pedigree of this fierce people, and persuade them that they are not sprung from a
nation in whose veins the blood of freedom
circulates.   The language in which they
would hear you tell them this tale would detect the imposition; your speech would betray
you.   An Englishman is the unfittest person
on earth to argue another Englishman into
slavery.

I think it is nearly as little in our power to
change their republican religion as their free

18. Arms remain to those who have been robbed.

descent; or to substitute tne Roman Catholic as a penalty, or the Church of England as an improvement. The mode of inquisition and dragooning is going out of fashion in the Old World, and I should not confide much to their efficacy in the New. The education of the Americans is also on the same unalterable bottom with their religion. You cannot persuade them to burn their books of curious science; to banish their lawyers from their courts of laws; or to quench the lights of their assemblies by refusing to choose those persons who are best read in their privileges. It would be no less impracticable to think of wholly annihilating the popular assemblies in which these lawyers sit. The army, by which we must govern in their place, would be far more chargeable to us, not quite so effectual, and perhaps in the end full as difficult to be kept in obedience.

With regard to the high aristocratic spirit of Virginia and the Southern Colonies, it has been proposed, I know, to reduce it by declaring a general enfranchisement of their slaves. This object has had its advocates and panegyrists; yet I never could argue myself into any opinion of it. Slaves are often much attached to their masters. A general wild offer of liberty would not always be accepted. History furnishes few instances of it. It is sometimes as hard to persuade slaves to be free, as it is to compel freemen to be slaves; and in this auspicious scheme we should have both these pleasing tasks on our hands at once. But when we talk of enfranchisement, do we not perceive that the American master may enfranchise too, and arm servile hands in defense of freedom?—a measure to which other people have had recourse more than once, and not without success, in a desperate situation of their affairs.

Slaves as these unfortunate black people are, and dull as all men are from slavery, must they not a little suspect the offer of freedom from that very nation which has sold them to their present masters? — from that nation, one of whose causes of quarrel with those masters is their refusal to deal any more in that inhuman traffic? An offer of freedom from England would come rather oddly, shipped to them in an African vessel which is refused an entry into the ports of Virginia or Carolina with a cargo of three hundred Angola negroes. It would be curious to see the Guinea captain attempting at the same instant to publish his proclamation of liberty, and to advertise his sale of slaves.

But let us suppose all these moral difficulties got over. The ocean remains. You cannot pump this dry; and as long as it continues in its present bed, so long all the causes which weaken authority by distance will continue.

"Ye gods, annihilate but space and time,
And make two lovers happy! "

was a pious and passionate prayer; but just as reasonable as many of the serious wishes of grave and solemn politicians.

If then, Sir, it seems almost desperate to think of any alternative course for changing the moral causes, and not quite easy to remove the natural, which produce prejudices irreconcilable to the late exercise of our authority — but that the spirit infallibly will continue, and, continuing, will produce such effects as now embarrass us — the second mode under consideration is to prosecute that spirit in its overt acts as criminal.

At this proposition I must pause a moment. The thing seems a great deal too big for my ideas of jurisprudence. It should seem to my way of conceiving such matters that there is a very wide difference, in reason and policy, between the mode of proceeding on the irregular conduct of scattered individuals, or even of bands of men who disturb order within the state, and the civil dissensions which may, from time to time, on great questions, agitate the several communities which compose a great empire. It looks to me to be narrow and pedantic to apply the ordinary ideas of criminal justice to this great public contest. I do not know the method of drawing up an indictment against a whole people. I cannot insult and ridicule the feelings of millions of my fellow-creatures as Sir Edward Coke [19] insulted one excellent individual (Sir Walter Raleigh) at the bar.[20] I hope I am not ripe to pass sentence on the gravest public bodies, intrusted with magistracies of great authority and dignity, and charged with the safety of their fellow-citizens, upon the very same title that I am. I really think that, for wise men, this is not judicious; for sober men, not decent; for minds tinctured with humanity, not mild and merciful.

Perhaps, Sir, I am mistaken in my idea of an empire, as distinguished from a single state or kingdom. But my idea of it is this, that

---

19. Attorney general in 1603.

20. "Coke: I will prove you the most notorious traitor that ever came to the bar.

Raleigh: Your words cannot condemn me. My innocency is my defense.

Coke: Thou art a monster. Thou hast an English face but a Spanish heart." Professor Goodrich from Howell's *State Trials*.

an empire is the aggregate of many states
under one common head, whether this head
be a monarch or a presiding republic. It
does, in such constitutions, frequently happen
—and nothing but the dismal, cold, dead uni-
formity of servitude can prevent its happen-
ing — that the subordinate parts have many
local privileges and immunities. Between
these privileges and the supreme common
authority the line may be extremely nice.
Of course disputes, often, too, very bitter
disputes, and much ill blood, will arise. But
though every privilege is an exemption, in
the case, from the ordinary exercise of the
supreme authority, it is no denial of it. The
claim of a privilege seems rather, *ex vi ter-
mini*,[21] to imply a superior power; for to talk
of the privileges of a state or of a person
who has no superior is hardly any better than
speaking nonsense.

Now, in such unfortunate quarrels among
the component parts of a great political
union of communities, I can scarcely conceive anything more completely imprudent
than for the head of the empire to insist that,
if any privilege is pleaded against his will or
his acts, his whole authority is denied; in-

---

21. By force of the term.

stantly to proclaim rebellion, to beat to arms, and to put the offending provinces under the ban. Will not this, Sir, very soon teach the provinces to make no distinctions on their part? Will it not teach them that the government, against which a claim of liberty is tantamount to high treason, is a government to which submission is equivalent to slavery? It may not always be quite convenient to impress dependent communities with such an idea.

We are, indeed, in all disputes with the Colonies, by the necessity of things, the judge. It is true, Sir. But I confess that the character of judge in my own cause is a thing that frightens me. Instead of filling me with pride, I am exceedingly humbled by it. I cannot proceed with a stern, assured, judicial conference until I find myself in something more like a judicial character. I must have these hesitations as long as I am compelled to recollect that, in my little reading upon such contests as these, the sense of mankind has at least as often decided against the superior as the subordinate power. Sir, let me add, too, that the opinion of my having some abstract right in my favor would not put me much at my ease in passing sentence, unless I could be sure that there were no rights which, in their exercise under certain circumstances, were not the most odious of all wrongs and the most vexatious of all injustice. Sir, these considerations have great weight with me when I find things so circumstanced, that I see the same party at once a civil litigant against me in point of right and a culprit before me, while I sit as a criminal judge on acts of his whose moral quality is to be decided upon the merits of that very litigation. Men are every now and then put, by the complexity of human affairs, into strange situations; but justice is the same, let the judge be in what situation he will.

There is, Sir, also a circumstance which convinces me that this mode of criminal proceeding is not, at least in the present stage of our contest, altogether expedient; which is nothing less than the conduct of those very persons who have seemed to adopt that mode by lately declaring a rebellion in Massachusetts Bay, as they had formerly addressed to have traitors brought hither, under an Act of Henry the Eighth, for trial. For though rebellion is declared, it is not proceeded against as such, nor have any steps been taken towards the apprehension or conviction of any individual offender, either on our late or our former Address; but modes of public coercion have been adopted, and such as have much more resemblance to a sort of qualified hostility toward an independent power than the punishment of rebellious subjects. All this seems rather inconsistent; but it shows how difficult it is to apply these juridical ideas to out present case.

In this situation, let us seriously and coolly ponder. What is it we have got by all our menaces, which have been many and ferocious? What advantage have we derived from the penal laws we have passed, and which, for the time, have been severe and numerous? What advances have we made towards our object by the sending of a force which, by land and sea, is no contemptible strength? Has the disorder abated? Nothing less. When I see things in this situation after such confident hopes, bold promises, and active exertions, I cannot, for my life, avoid a suspicion that the plan itself is not correctly right.

If, then, the removal of the causes of this spirit of American liberty be for the greater part, or rather entirely, impracticable; if the ideas of criminal process be inapplicable — or, if applicable, are in the highest degree inexpedient; what way yet remains? No way is open but the third and last,— to comply with the American spirit as necessary; or, if you please, to submit to it as a necessary evil.

If we adopt this mode,— if we mean to conciliate and concede,— let us see of what nature the concession ought to be. To ascertain the nature of our concession, we must look at their complaint. The Colonies complain that they have not the characteristic mark and seal of British freedom. They complain that they are taxed in a Parliament in which they are not represented. If you mean to satisfy them at all, you must satisfy them with regard to this complaint. If you mean to please any people, you must give them the boon which they ask; not what you may think better for them, but of a kind totally different. Such an act may be a wise regulation, but it is no concession; whereas our present theme is the mode of giving satisfaction.

Sir, I think you must perceive that I am resolved this day to have nothing at all to do with the question of the right of taxation. Some gentlemen startle — but it is true; I put it totally out of the question. It is less than nothing in my consideration. I do not indeed wonder, nor will you, Sir, that gentlemen of profound learning are fond of displaying it on this profound subject. But my consideration is narrow, confined, and wholly limited to the policy of the question. I do not examine whether the giving away a man's money be a power excepted and reserved out of the general trust of government, and how far all mankind, in all forms of polity, are entitled to an exercise of that right by the charter of nature; or whether, on the contrary, a right of taxation is necessarily involved in the general principle of legislation, and inseparable from the ordinary supreme power. These are deep questions, where great names militate against each other, where reason is perplexed, and an appeal to authorities only thickens the confusion; for high and reverend authorities lift up their heads on both sides, and there is no sure footing in the middle. This point is the great

> "Serbonian bog,
> Betwixt Damiata and Mount Casius old,
> Where armies whole have sunk." [22]

I do not intend to be overwhelmed in that bog, though in such respectable company.

---

22. From *Paradise Lost.*

The question with me is, not whether you have a right to render your people miserable, but whether it is not your interest to make them happy. It is not what a lawyer tells me I *may* do, but what humanity, reason, and justice tell me I *ought* to do. Is a politic act the worse for being a generous one? Is no concession proper but that which is made from your want of right to keep what you grant? Or does it lessen the grace or dignity of relaxing in the exercise of an odious claim because you have your evidence-room full of titles, and your magazine stuffed with arms to enforce them? What signify all those titles, and all those arms? Of what avail are they when the reason of the thing tells me that the assertion of my title is the loss of my suit, and that I could do nothing but wound myself by the use of my own weapons?

Such is steadfastly my opinion of the absolute necessity of keeping up the concord of this Empire by a unity of spirit, though in a diversity of operations, that, if I were sure the Colonists had, at their leaving this country, sealed a regular compact of servitude; that they had solemnly abjured all the rights of citizens; that they had made a vow to renounce all ideas of liberty for them and their posterity to all generations; yet I should hold myself obliged to conform to the temper I found universally prevalent in my own day, and to govern two million of men, impatient of servitude, on the principles of freedom. I am not determining a point of law, I am restoring tranquillity ; and the general character and situation of a people must determine what sort of government is fitted for them. That point nothing else can or ought to determine.

My idea, therefore, without considering whether we yield as matter of right, or grant as matter of favor, is to admit the people of our Colonies into an interest in the Constitution; and, by recording that admission in the journals of Parliament, to give them as strong an assurance as the nature of the thing will admit, that we mean forever to adhere to that solemn declaration of systematic indulgence.

Some years ago the repeal of a revenue act might have served to show that we intended an unconditional abatement of the exercise of a taxing power. Such a measure was then sufficient to remove all suspicion, and to give perfect content. But unfortunate events since that time may make something further necessary; and not more necessary for the satisfaction of the Colonies than for the dignity and consistency of our own future proceedings.

I have taken a very incorrect measure of the disposition of the House if this proposal in itself would be received with dislike. I think, Sir, we have few American financiers. But our misfortune is, we are too acute, we are too exquisite in our conjectures of the future, for men oppressed with such great and present evils. The more moderate among the opposers of Parliamentary concession freely confess that they hope no good from taxation, but they apprehend the Colonists have further views; and if this point were conceded, they would instantly attack the trade laws. These gentlemen are convinced that this was the intention from the beginning, and the quarrel of the Americans with taxation was no more than a cloak and cover to this design. Such has been the language even of a gentleman of real moderation, and of a natural temper well adjusted to fair and equal government.[23] I am, however, Sir, not a little surprised at this kind of discourse, whenever I hear it; and I am the more surprised on account of the arguments which I constantly find in company with it, and which are often urged from the same mouths and on the same day.

For instance, when we allege that it is

---

23. Mr. Rice.

against reason to tax a people under so many restraints in trade as the Americans, the noble lord in the blue ribbon shall tell you that the restraints on trade are futile and useless — of no advantage to us, and of no burthen to those on whom they are imposed; that the trade to America is not secured by the Acts of Navigation, but by the natural and irresistible advantage of a commercial preference.

Such is the merit of the trade laws in this posture of the debate. But when strong internal circumstances are urged against the taxes; when the scheme is dissected; when experience and the nature of things are brought to prove, and do prove, the utter impossibility of obtaining an effective revenue from the Colonies; when these things are pressed, or rather press themselves, so as to drive the advocates of Colony taxes to a clear admission of the futility of the scheme; then, Sir, the sleeping trade laws revive from their trance, and this useless taxation is to be kept sacred, not for its own sake, but as a counter-guard and security of the laws of trade.

Then, Sir, you keep up revenue laws which are mischievous, in order to preserve trade laws that are useless. Such is the wisdom of our plan in both its members. They are sep-

THE BRIDGE

arately given up as of no value, and yet one is always to be defended for the sake of the other; but I cannot agree with the noble lord, nor with the pamphlet from whence he seems to have borrowed these ideas concerning the inutility of the trade laws. For, without idolizing them, I am sure they are still, in many ways, of great use to us; and in former times they have been of the greatest. They do confine, and they do greatly narrow, the market for the Americans; but my perfect conviction of this does not help me in the least to discern how the revenue laws form any security whatsoever to the commercial regulations, or that these commercial regulations are the true ground of the quarrel, or that the giving way, in any one instance of authority, is to lose all that may remain unconceded.

One fact is clear and undisputable. The public and avowed origin of this quarrel was on taxation. This quarrel has indeed brought on new disputes on new questions; but certainly the least bitter, and the fewest of all, on the trade laws. To judge which of the two be the real radical cause of quarrel, we have to see whether the commercial dispute did, in order of time, precede the dispute on taxation. There is not a shadow of evidence for it.   Next, to enable us to judge whether at this moment a dislike to the trade laws be the real cause of quarrel, it is absolutely necessary to put the taxes out of the question by a repeal.   See how the Americans act in this position, and then you will be able to discern correctly what is the true object of the controversy, or whether any controversy at all will remain.   Unless you consent to remove this cause of difference, it is impossible, with decency, to assert that the dispute is not upon what it is avowed to be.   And I would, Sir, recommend to your serious consideration whether it be prudent to form a rule for punishing people, not on their own acts, but on your conjectures?   Surely it is preposterous at the very best.   It is not justifying your anger by their misconduct, but it is converting your ill-will into their delinquency.

But the Colonies will go further. Alas! alas! when will this speculation against fact and reason end?   What will quiet these panic fears which we entertain of the hostile effect of a conciliatory conduct?   Is it true that no case can exist in which it is proper for the sovereign to accede to the desires of his discontented subjects?   Is there anything peculiar in this case to make a rule for itself?   Is all authority of course lost when it is not pushed to the extreme? Is it a certain maxim that the fewer causes of dissatisfaction are left by government, the more the subject will be inclined to resist and rebel?

All these objections being in fact no more than suspicions, conjectures, divinations, formed in defiance of fact and experience, they did not, Sir, discourage me from entertaining the idea of a conciliatory concession founded on the principles which I have just stated.

In forming a plan for this purpose, I endeavored to put myself in that frame of mind which was the most natural and the most reasonable, and which was certainly the most probable means of securing me from all error. I set out with a perfect distrust of my own abilities, a total renunciation of every speculation of my own, and with a profound reverence for the wisdom of our ancestors who have left us the inheritance of so happy a Constitution and so flourishing an empire, and, what is a thousand times more valuable, the treasury of the maxims and principles which formed the one and obtained the other.

During the reigns of the kings of Spain of the Austrian family, whenever they were at a loss in the Spanish councils, it was common for their statesmen to say that they ought to consult the genius of Philip the Second. The genius of Philip the Second might mislead them, and the issue of their affairs showed that they had not chosen the most perfect standard; but, Sir, I am sure that I shall not be misled when, in a case of constitutional difficulty, I consult the genius of the English Constitution. Consulting at that oracle — it was with all due humility and piety — I found four capital examples in a similar case before me; those of Ireland, Wales, Chester, and Durham.

Ireland, before the English conquest, though never governed by a despotic power, had no Parliament. How far the English Parliament itself was at that time modeled according to the present form is disputed among antiquaries; but we have all the reason in the world to be assured that a form of Parliament such as England then enjoyed she instantly communicated to Ireland, and we are equally sure that almost every successive improvement in constitutional liberty, as fast as it was made here, was transmitted thither. The feudal baronage and the feudal knighthood, the roots of our primitive Constitution, were early transplanted into that soil, and grew and flourished there. Magna Charta, if it did not give us originally the House of Commons, gave us at least a House of Commons of weight and consequence. But your ancestors did not churlishly sit down alone to the feast of Magna Charta. Ireland was made immediately a partaker. This benefit of English laws and liberties, I confess, was not at first extended to all Ireland. Mark the consequence. English authority and English liberties had exactly the same boundaries. Your standard could never be advanced an inch before your privileges.[24] Sir John Davis shows beyond a doubt that the refusal of a general communication of these rights was the true cause why Ireland was five hundred years in subduing; and after the vain projects of a military government, attempted in the reign of Queen Elizabeth, it was soon discovered that nothing could make that country English, in civility and allegiance, but your laws and your forms of legislature. It was not English arms, but the English Constitution, that conquered Ireland. From that time Ireland has ever had a general Parlia-

---

24. English settlers in Ireland after the invasion of Strongbow kept themselves, within certain limits, distinct from the natives, called the "Pale." They enjoyed English law while the natives were denied it. —*Professor Goodrich.*

ment, as she had before a partial Parliament. You changed the people; you altered the religion; but you never touched the form or the vital substance of free government in that Kingdom. You deposed kings; you restored them; you altered the succession to theirs, as well as to your own Crown; but you never altered their Constitution, the principle of which was respected by usurpation, restored with the restoration of monarchy, and established, I trust, forever, by the glorious Revolution. This has made Ireland the great and flourishing kingdom that it is,[25] and, from a disgrace and a burthen intolerable to this nation, has rendered her a principal part of our strength and ornament. This country cannot be said to have ever formally taxed her. The irregular things done in the confusion of mighty troubles and on the hinge of great revolutions, even if all were done that is said to have been done, form no example. If they have any effect in argument, they make an exception to prove the rule. None of your own liberties could stand a moment, if the casual deviations from them at such times were suffered to be used as proofs of their nullity. By the lucrative amount of such casual breaches in the

25. A somewhat exaggerated statmeent.

constitution, judge what the stated and fixed rule of supply has been in that kingdom. Your Irish pensioners would starve, if they had no other fund to live on than taxes granted by English authority. Turn your eyes to those popular grants from whence all your great supplies are come, and learn to respect that only source of public wealth in the British Empire.

My next example is Wales. This country is said to be reduced by Henry the Third. It was said more truly to be so by Edward the First. But though then conquered, it was not looked upon as any part of the realm of England. Its old Constitution, whatever that might have been, was destroyed, and no good one was substituted in its place. The care of that tract was put into the hands of Lords Marchers — a form of government of a very singular kind; a strange heterogeneous monster, something between hostility and government; perhaps it has a sort of resemblance, according to the modes of those terms, to that of Commander-in-chief at present, to whom all civil power is granted as secondary. The manners of the Welsh nation followed the genius of the government. The people were ferocious, restive, savage, and uncultivated;

sometimes composed, never pacified. Wales, within itself, was in perpetual disorder, and it kept the frontier of England in perpetual alarm. Benefits from it to the state there were none. Wales was only known to England by incursion and invasion.

Sir, during that state of things, Parliament was not idle. They attempted to subdue the fierce spirit of the Welsh by all sorts of rigorous laws. They prohibited by statute the sending of all sorts of arms into Wales, as you prohibit by proclamation (with something more of doubt on the legality) the sending of arms to America. They disarmed the Welsh by statute, as you attempted (but still with more question on the legality) to disarm New England by an instruction. They made an Act to drag offenders from Wales into England for trial, as you have done (but with more hardship) with regard to America. By another Act, where one of the parties was an Englishman, they ordained that his trial should be always by English. They made Acts to restrain trade, as you do; and they prevented the Welsh from the use of fairs and markets, as you do the Americans from fisheries and foreign ports. In short, when the Statute Book was not quite so much swelled as it is now, you find no less than fifteen acts of penal regulation on the subject of Wales.

Here we rub our hands.—A fine body of precedents for the authority of Parliament and the use of it!—I admit it fully; and pray add likewise to these precedents that all the while Wales rid this Kingdom like an incubus, that it was an unprofitable and oppressive burthen, and that an Englishman traveling in that country could not go six yards from the high road without being murdered.

The march of the human mind is slow. Sir, it was not until after two hundred years discovered that, by an eternal law, Providence had decreed vexation to violence, and poverty to rapine. Your ancestors did however at length open their eyes to the ill-husbandry of injustice. They found that the tyranny of a free people could of all tyrannies the least be endured, and that laws made against a whole nation were not the most effectual methods of securing its obedience. Accordingly, in the twenty-seventh year of Henry the Eighth the course was entirely altered. With a preamble stating the entire and perfect rights of the Crown of England, it gave to the Welsh all the rights and privileges of English subjects. A political order was established; the military power gave way to the civil; the Marches were turned into Counties. But that a nation should have a right to English liberties, and yet no share at all in the fundamental security of these liberties — the grant of their own property — seemed a thing so incongruous, that, eight years after, that is, in the thirty-fifth of that reign, a complete and not ill-proportioned representation by counties and boroughs was bestowed upon Wales by Act of Parliament. From that moment, as by a charm, the tumults subsided; obedience was restored; peace, order, and civilization followed in the train of liberty. When the day-star of the English Constitution had arisen in their hearts, all was harmony within and without —

> "— simul alba nautis
> Stella refulsit,
> Defluit saxis agitatus humor;
> Concidunt venti, fugiuntque nubes,
> Et minax (quod sic voluere) ponto
> Unda recumbit." [26]

The very same year the County Palatine of Chester received the same relief from its op-

---

26. The troubled surge falls from the rocks, the winds cease, the clouds vanish and the threatening waves subside in the seas as the clear constellation shines forth.

pressions and the same remedy to its disorders. Before this time Chester was little less distempered than Wales. The inhabitants, without rights themselves, were the fittest to destroy the rights of others; and from thence Richard the Second drew the standing army of archers with which for a time he oppressed England. The people of Chester applied to Parliament in a petition penned as I shall read to you:—

"To the King, our Sovereign Lord, in most humble wise shewen unto your excellent Majesty the inhabitants of your Grace's County Palatine or Chester: (1) That where the said County Palatine of Chester is and hath been always hitherto exempt, excluded, and separated out and from your High Court of Parliament, to have any Knights and Burgesses within the said Court; by reason whereof the said inhabitants have hitherto sustained manifold disherisons, losses, and damages, as well in their lands, goods, and bodies, as in the good, civil, and politic governance and maintenance of the commonwealth of their said county; (2) And forasmuch as the said inhabitants have always hitherto been bound by the Acts and Statutes made and ordained by your said Highness and your most

noble progenitors, by authority of the said
Court, as far forth as other counties, cities,
and boroughs have been, that have had their
Knights and Burgesses within your said Court
of Parliament, and yet have had neither
Knight ne Burgess there for the said County
Palatine; the said inhabitants for lack thereof,
have been oftentimes touched and grieved
with Acts and Statutes made within the said
Court, as well derogatory unto the most
ancient jurisdictions, liberties, and privileges
of your said County Palatine, as prejudicial
unto the commonwealth, quietness, rest, and
peace of your Grace's most bounden subjects
inhabiting within the same."

What did Parliament with this audacious
address?—Reject it as a libel? Treat it as
an affront to Government? Spurn it as a
derogation from the rights of legislature? Did
they toss it over the table? Did they burn it
by the hands of the common hangman? They
took the petition of grievance, all rugged as
it was, without softening or temperament,
unpurged of the original bitterness and indig-
nation of complaint — they made it the very
preamble to their Act of Redress, and couse-
crated its principle to all ages in the sanctuary
of legislation.

Here is my third example. It was attended with the success of the two former. Chester, civilized as well as Wales, has demonstrated that freedom, and not servitude, is the cure of anarchy; as religion, and not atheism, is the true remedy for superstition. Sir, this pattern of Chester was followed in the reign of Charles the Second with regard to the County Palatine of Durham, which is my fourth example. This county had long lain out of the pale of free legislation. So scrupulously was the example of Chester followed that the style of the preamble is nearly the same with that of the Chester Act; and, without affecting the abstract extent of the authority of Parliament, it recognizes the equity of not suffering any considerable district in which the British subjects may act as a body, to be taxed without their own voice in the grant.

Now if the doctrines of policy contained in these preambles, and the force of these examples in the Acts of Parliaments, avail anything, what can be said against applying them with regard to America? Are not the people of America as much Englishmen as the Welsh? The preamble of the Act of Henry the Eighth says the Welsh speak a language no way resembling that of his Majesty's

English subjects. Are the Americans not as numerous? If we may trust the learned and accurate Judge Barrington's account of North Wales, and take that as a standard to measure the rest, there is no comparison. The people cannot amount to above 200,000; not a tenth part of the number in the Colonies. Is America in rebellion? Wales was hardly ever free from it. Have you attempted to govern America by penal statutes? You made fifteen for Wales. But your legislative authority is perfect with regard to America. Was it less perfect in Wales, Chester, and Durham? But America is virtually represented. What! does the electric force of virtual representation more easily pass over the Atlantic than pervade Wales, which lies in your neighborhood —or than Chester and Durham, surrounded by abundance of representation that is actual and palpable? But, Sir, your ancestors thought this sort of virtual representation, however ample, to be totally insufficient for the freedom of the inhabitants of territories that are so near, and comparatively so inconsiderable. How then can I think it sufficient for those which are infinitely greater, and infinitely more remote.

You will now, Sir, perhaps imagine that I

am on the point of proposing to you a scheme for a representation of the Colonies in Parliament. Perhaps I might be inclined to entertain some such thought; but a great flood stops me in my course. *Opposuit natura.* [27] — I cannot remove the eternal barriers of the creation. The thing, in that mode, I do not know to be possible. As I meddle with no theory, I do not absolutely assert the impracticability of such a representation; but I do not see my way to it, and those who have been more confident have not been more successful. However, the arm of public benevolence is not shortened, and there are often several means to the same end. What nature has disjoined in one way, wisdom may unite in another. When we cannot give the benefit as we would wish, let us not refuse it altogether. If we cannot give the principal, let us find a substitute. But how? Where? What substitute?

Fortunately I am not obliged, for the ways and means of this substitute, to tax my own unproductive invention. I am not even obliged to go to the rich treasury of the fertile framers of imaginary commonwealths— not to the Republic of Plato, not to the Utopia of

---

27. Nature opposes it.

More, not to the Oceana of Harrington. It is before me — it is at my feet,

> " And the rude swain
> Treads daily on it with his clouted shoon."

I only wish you to recognize, for the theory, the ancient constitutional policy of this kingdom with regard to representation, as that policy has been declared in Acts of Parliament; and as to the practice, to return to that mode which a uniform experience has marked out to you as best, and in which you walked with security, advantage, and honor, until the year 1763.

My resolutions therefore mean to establish the equity and justice of a taxation of America by *grant*, and not by *imposition;* to mark the *legal competency* of the Colony Assemblies for the support of their government in peace, and for public aids in time of war; to acknowledge that this legal competency has had a *dutiful and beneficial exercise;* and that experience has shown the *benefit of their grants*, and the *futility of Parliamentary taxation* as a method of supply.

These solid truths compose six fundamental propositions. There are three more resolutions corollary to these. If you admit the first set, you can hardly reject the others. But if you admit the first, I shall be far from solicitous whether you accept or refuse the last. I think these six massive pillars will be of strength sufficient to support the temple of British concord. I have no more doubt than I entertain of my existence that, if you admitted these, you would command an immediate peace, and, with but tolerable future management, a lasting obedience in America. I am not arrogant in this confident assurance. The propositions are all mere matters of fact, and if they are such facts as draw irresistible conclusions even in the stating, this is the power of truth, and not any management of mine.

Sir, I shall open the whole plan to you, together with such observations on the motions as may tend to illustrate them where they may want explanation. The first is a resolution —

"That the Colonies and Plantations of Great Britain in North America, consisting of fourteen separate Governments, and containing two millions and upwards of free inhabitants, have not had the liberty and privilege of electing and sending any Knights and Burgesses, or others, to represent them in the High Court of Parliament."

This is a plain matter of fact, necessary to be laid down, and, excepting the description, it is laid down in the language of the Constitution; it is taken nearly *verbatim* from acts of Parliament.

The second is like unto the first —

"That the said Colonies and Plantations have been liable to, and bounden by, several subsidies, payments, rates, and taxes given and granted by Parliament, though the said Colonies and Plantations have not their Knights and Burgesses in the said High Court of Parliament, of their own election, to represent the condition of their country; by lack whereof they have been oftentimes touched and grieved by subsidies given, granted, and assented to, in the said Court, in a manner prejudicial to the commonwealth, quietness, rest, and peace of the subjects inhabiting within the same."

Is this description too hot, or too cold; too strong, or too weak? Does it arrogate too much to the supreme legislature? Does it lean too much to the claims of the people? If it runs into any of these errors, the fault is not mine. It is the language of your own ancient Acts of Parliament.

"Non meus hic sermo, sed quæ præcepit Ofellus,
  Rusticus, abnormis sapiens."[28]

It is the genuine product of the ancient, rustic, manly, homebred sense of this country. —I did not dare to rub off a particle of the venerable rust that rather adorns and preserves, than destroys, the metal. It would be a profanation to touch with a tool the stones which construct this sacred altar of peace. I would not violate with modern polish the ingenuous and noble roughness of these truly constitutional materials. Above all things, I was resolved not to be guilty of tampering, the odious vice of restless and unstable minds. I put my foot in the tracks of our forefathers, where I can neither wander nor stumble. Determining to fix articles of peace, I was resolved not to be wise beyond what was written; I was resolved to use nothing else than the form of sound words, to let others abound in their own sense, and carefully to abstain from all expressions of my own. What the law has said, I say. In all things else I am silent. I have no organ but for her words. This, if it be not ingenious, I am sure is safe.

---

28. This is no creed of mine, but what Ofellus the peasant philosopher taught me.

There are indeed words expressive of grievance in this second resolution, which those who are resolved always to be in the right will deny to contain matter of fact, as applied to the present case, although Parliament thought them true with regard to the counties of Chester and Durham.   They will deny that the Americans were ever "touched and grieved" with the taxes. If they consider nothing in taxes but their weight as pecuniary impositions, there might be some pretense for this denial; but men may be sorely touched and deeply grieved in their privileges, as well as in their purses.   Men may lose little in property by the act which takes away all their freedom.   When a man is robbed of a trifle on the highway, it is not the two-pence lost that constitutes the capital outrage.   This is not confined to privileges.   Even ancient indulgences, withdrawn without offense on the part of those who enjoyed such favors, operate as grievances.   But were the Americans then not touched and grieved by the taxes, in some measure, merely as taxes?   If so, why were they almost all either wholly repealed, or exceedingly reduced?   Were they not touched and grieved even by the regulating duties of the sixth of George the Second?   Else, why were the duties first reduced to one-third in 1764, and afterwards to a third of that third in the year 1766? Were they not touched and grieved by the Stamp Act? I shall say they were, until that tax is revived. Were they not touched and grieved by the duties of 1767, which were likewise repealed, and which Lord Hillsborough tells you, for the Ministry, were laid contrary to the true principle of commerce? Is not the assurance given by that noble person to the Colonies of a resolution to lay no more taxes on them an admission that taxes would touch and grieve them? Is not the resolution of the noble lord in the blue ribbon, now standing on your Journals, the strongest of all proofs that Parliamentary subsidies really touched and grieved them? Else why all these changes, modifications, repeals, assurances, and resolutions?

The next proposition is —

"That, from the distance of the said Colonies, and from other circumstances, no method had hitherto been devised for procuring a representation in Parliament for the said Colonies."

This is an assertion of a fact. I go no further on the paper, though, in my private judgment, a useful representation is impossible — I am sure it is not desired by them, nor ought it perhaps by us — but I abstain from opinions.

The fourth resolution is —

"That each of the said Colonies hath within itself a body, chosen in part, or in the whole, by the freemen, freeholders, or other free inhabitants thereof, commonly called the General Assembly, or General Court, with powers legally to raise, levy, and assess, according to the several usage of such Colonies, duties and taxes towards defraying all sorts of public services."

This competence in the Colony Assemblies is certain. It is proved by the whole tenor of their Acts of Supply in all the Assemblies, in which the constant style of granting is, "an aid to his Majesty;" and Acts granting to the Crown have regularly for nearly a century passed the public offices without dispute. Those who have been pleased paradoxically to deny this right, holding that none but the British Parliament can grant to the Crown, are wished to look to what is done, not only in the Colonies, but in Ireland, in one uniform unbroken tenor every session. Sir, I am surprised that this doctrine should come from some of the law servants of the Crown.

I say that if the Crown could be responsible, his Majesty,—but certainly the Ministers,— and even these law officers themselves through whose hands the Acts passed, biennially in Ireland, or annually in the Colonies — are in an habitual course of committing impeachable offenses. What habitual offenders have been all Presidents of the Council, all Secretaries of State, all First Lords of Trade, all Attorneys and all Solicitors-General! However, they are safe, as no one impeaches them; and there is no ground of charge against them except in their own unfounded theories.

The fifth resolution is also a resolution of fact—

"That the said General Assemblies, General Courts, or other bodies legally qualified as aforesaid, have at sundry times freely granted several large subsidies and public aids for his Majesty's service, according to their abilities, when required thereto by letter from one of his Majesty's principal Secretaries of State; and that their right to grant the same, and their cheerfulness and sufficiency in the said grants, have been at sundry times acknowledged by Parliament."

To say nothing of their great expenses in the Indian wars, and not to take their exertion in foreign ones so high as the supplies in the year 1695 — not to go back to their public contributions in the year 1710 — I shall begin to travel only where the journals give me light, resolving to deal in nothing but fact, authenticated by Parliamentary record, and to build myself wholly on that solid basis.

On the 4th of April, 1748, a committee of this House came to the following resolution:

"Resolved: That it is the opinion of this Committee that it is just and reasonable that the several Provinces and Colonies of Massachusetts Bay, New Hampshire, Connecticut, and Rhode Island be reimbursed the expenses they have been at in taking and securing to the Crown of Great Britain the Island of Cape Breton and its dependencies."

The expenses were immense for such Colonies. They were above £200,000 sterling; money first raised and advanced on their public credit.

On the 28th of January, 1756, a message from the King came to us, to this effect:

"His Majesty, being sensible of the zeal and vigor with which his faithful subjects of certain Colonies in North America have exerted themselves in defense of his Majesty's just rights and possessions, recommends it to this House to take the same into their consideration, and to enable his Majesty to give them such assistance as may be a proper reward and encouragement."

On the 3d of February, 1756, the House came to a suitable resolution, expressed in words nearly the same as those of the message, but with the further addition, that the money then voted was as an encouragement to the Colonies to exert themselves with vigor. It will not be necessary to go through all the testimonies which your own records have given to the truth of my resolutions. I will only refer you to the places in the Journals:

Vol. xxvii.— 16th and 19th May, 1757.
Vol. xxviii.— June 1st, 1758; April 26th
and 30th, 1759; March 26th and
31st, and April 28th, 1760; Jan.
9th and 20th, 1761.
Vol. xxix. — Jan. 22d and 26th, 1762;
March 14th and 17th, 1763.

Sir, here is the repeated acknowledgment of Parliament that the colonies not only gave, but gave to satiety. This nation has formally acknowledged two things: first, that the Colonies had gone beyond their abilities, Parliament having thought it necessary to reimburse them; secondly, that they had acted legally and laudably in their grants of money, and their maintenance of troops, since the compensation is expressly given as reward and encouragement. Reward is not bestowed for acts that are unlawful; and encouragement is not held out to things that deserve reprehension. My resolution therefore does nothing more than collect into one proposition what is scattered through your Journals. I give you nothing but your own; and you cannot refuse in the gross what you have so often acknowledged in detail. The admission of this, which will be so honorable to them and to you, will, indeed, be mortal to all the miserable stories by which the passions of the misguided people have been engaged in an unhappy system. The people heard, indeed, from the beginning of these disputes, one thing continually dinned in their ears, that reason and justice demanded that the Americans, who paid no taxes, should be compelled to contribute. How did that fact of their paying nothing stand when the taxing system began? When Mr. Grenville began to form his system of American revenue, he stated in this house that the Colonies were then in debt

two millions six hundred thousand pounds
sterling money, and was of opinion they would
discharge that debt in four years. On this
statement, those untaxed people were actually
subject to the payment of taxes to the amount
of six hundred and fifty thousand a year. In
fact, however, Mr. Grenville was mistaken.
The funds given for sinking the debt did not
prove quite so ample as both the Colonies and
he expected. The calculation was too sanguine; the reduction was not completed till
some years after, and at different times in different Colonies. However, the taxes after the
war continued too great to bear any addition,
with prudence or propriety; and when the
burthens imposed in consequence of former
requisitions were discharged, our tone became
too high to resort again to requisition. No
Colony, since that time, ever has had any
requisition whatsoever made to it.

We see the sense of the Crown, and the
sense of Parliament, on the productive nature
of a *revenue by grant*. Now search the same
Journals for the produce of the *revenue by imposition*. Where is it? Let us know the volume and the page. What is the gross, what
is the net produce? To what service is it applied? How have you appropriated its sur-

plus? What! Can none of the many skillful index-makers that we are now employing find any trace of it?—Well, let them and that rest together. But are the Journals, which say nothing of the revenue, as silent on the discontent? Oh no! a child may find it. It is the melancholy burthen and blot of every page.

I think, then, I am, from those Journals, justified in the sixth and last resolution, which is—

"That it hath been found by experience that the manner of granting the said supplies and aids, by the said General Assemblies, hath been more agreeable to the said Colonies, and more beneficial and conducive to the public service, than the mode of giving and granting aids in Parliament, to be raised and paid in the said Colonies."

This makes the whole of the fundamental part of the plan. The conclusion is irresistible. You cannot say that you were driven by any necessity to an exercise of the utmost rights of legislature. You cannot assert that you took on yourself the task of imposing Colony taxes from the want of another legal body that is competent to the purpose of supplying the exigencies of the state without wounding the prejudices of the people. Neither is it true that the body so qualified, and having that competence, had neglected the duty.

The question now, on all this accumulated matter, is : whether you will choose to abide by a profitable experience, or a mischievous theory; whether you choose to build on imagination, or fact; whether you prefer enjoyment, or hope; satisfaction in your subjects, or discontent ?

If these propositions are accepted, everything which has been made to enforce a contrary system must, I take it for granted, fall along with it. On that ground, I have drawn the following resolution, which, when it comes to be moved, will naturally be divided in a proper manner :

"That it may be proper to repeal an Act made in the seventh year of the reign of his present Majesty, entitled, An Act for granting certain duties in the British Colonies and Plantations in America; for allowing a drawback of the duties of customs upon the exportation from this Kingdom of coffee and cocoa-nuts of the produce of the said Colonies or Plantations; for discontinuing the drawbacks payable on china earthenware exported to America; and for more effectually preventing the clandestine running of goods in the said Colonies and Plantations. And that it may be proper to repeal an Act made in the fourteenth year of the reign of his present Majesty, entitled, An Act to discontinue, in such manner and for such time as are therein mentioned, the landing and discharging, lading or shipping of goods, wares, and merchandise at the town and within the harbor of Boston, in the Province of Massachusetts Bay, in North America. And that it may be proper to repeal an Act made in the fourteenth year of the reign of his present Majesty, entitled, An Act for the impartial administration of justice in the cases of persons questioned for any acts done by them in the execution of the law, or for the suppression of riots and tumults, in the Province of Massachusetts Bay, in New England. And that it may be proper to repeal an Act made in the fourteenth year of the reign of his present Majesty, entitled, An Act for the better regulating of the Government of the Province of the Massachusetts Bay, in New England. And also that it may be proper to explain and amend an Act made in the thirty-fifth year of the reign of King Henry the Eighth, entitled, An Act for the Trial of Treasons committed out of the King's Dominions."

I wish, Sir, to repeal the Boston Port Bill, because — independently of the dangerous precedent of suspending the rights of the subject during the King's pleasure — it was passed, as I apprehend, with less regularity and on more partial principles than it ought. The corporation of Boston was not heard before it was condemned. Other towns, full as guilty as she was, have not had their ports blocked up. Even the Restraining Bill of the present session does not go to the length of the Boston Port Act. The same ideas of prudence which induced you not to extend equal punishment to equal guilt, even when you were punishing, induced me, who mean not to chastise, but to reconcile, to be satisfied with the punishment already partially inflicted.

Ideas of prudence and accommodation to circumstances prevent you from taking away the charters of Connecticut and Rhode Island, as you have taken away that of Massachusetts Bay, though the Crown has far less power in the two former provinces than it enjoyed in the latter, and though the abuses have been full as great, and as flagrant, in the exempted as in the punished. The same reasons of prudence and accommodation have weight with me in restoring the charter of Massachusetts Bay. Besides, Sir, the Act which changes the charter of Massachusetts is in many particulars so exceptionable that if I did not wish absolutely to repeal, I would by all means desire to alter it, as several of its provisions tend to the subversion of all public and private justice. Such, among others, is the power in the Governor to change the sheriff at his pleasure, and to make a new returning officer for every special cause. It is shameful to behold such a regulation standing among English laws.

The Act for bringing persons accused of committing murder, under the orders of Government to England for trial, is but temporary. That Act has calculated the probable duration of our quarrel with the Colonies, and is accommodated to that supposed duration. I would hasten the happy moment of reconciliation, and therefore must, on my principle, get rid of that most justly obnoxious Act.

The Act of Henry the Eighth, for the Trial of Treasons, I do not mean to take away, but to confine it to its proper bounds and original intention; to make it expressly for trial of treasons—and the greatest treasons may be committed—in places where the jurisdiction of the Crown does not extend.

Having guarded the privileges of local legislature, I would next secure to the Colonies a fair and unbiased judicature, for which purpose, Sir, I propose the following resolution:

"That, from the time when the General Assembly or General Court of any Colony or Plantation in North America shall have appointed by Act of Assembly, duly confirmed, a settled salary to the offices of the Chief Justice and other Judges of the Superior Court, it may be proper that the said Chief Justice and other Judges of the Superior Courts of such Colony shall hold his and their office and offices during their good behavior, and shall not be removed therefrom but when the said removal shall be adjudged by his Majesty in Council, upon a hearing on complaint from the General Assembly, or a complaint from the Governor, or Council, or the House of Representatives severally, or of the Colony in which the said Chief Justice and other Judges have exercised the said offices."

The next resolution relates to the Courts of Admiralty. It is this:

"That it may be proper to regulate the Courts of Admiralty or Vice-Admiralty authorized by the Fifteenth Chapter of the Fourth of George the Third, in such a manner as to make the same more commodious to those who sue, or are sued, in the said Courts, and to provide for the more decent maintenance of the Judges in the same."

These courts I do not wish to take away; they are in themselves proper establishments. This court is one of the capital securities of the Act of Navigation. The extent of its jurisdiction, indeed, has been increased, but this is altogether as proper, and is indeed on many accounts more eligible, where new powers were wanted, than a court absolutely new. But courts incommodiously situated, in effect, deny justice; and a court partaking in the fruits of its own condemnation is a robber. The Congress complain, and complain justly, of this grievance.

These are the three consequential propositions. I have thought of two or three more, but they come rather too near detail, and to the province of executive government, which I wish Parliament always to superintend, never to assume. If the first six are granted, congruity will carry the latter three. If not, the things that remain unrepealed will be, I hope, rather unseemly incumbrances on the building, than very materially detrimental to its strength and stability.

Here, Sir, I should close; but I plainly perceive some objections remain which I ought, if possible, to remove.

[Here Burke answers the objection that the colonies will abuse the privileges given them and throw off their allegiance. His central idea is in the words: "In every arduous enterprise we consider what we are to lose, as well as what we are to gain; and the more and better stake of liberty every people possess, the less they will hazard in a vain attempt to make it more. These are the cords of man. Man acts from adequate motives relative to his interest, and not on metaphysical speculations."

He then proceeds to criticise and to overthrow by a series of arguments a proposition that had recently been brought forward by Lord North. This discussion would extend over several printed pages and is the only considerable omission we make. In the end he compares his plan with Lord North's in these words:

"This I offer to give you is plain and simple; the other full of perplexed and intricate mazes. This is mild; that is harsh. This is found by experience effectual for its purposes; the other is a new project. This is universal; the other calculated for certain Colonies only. This is immediate in its conciliatory operation; the other remote, contingent, full of hazard. Mine is what becomes the dignity of a feeling people — gratuitous, unconditional, and not held out as a matter of bargain and sale."]

But what, says the financier, is peace to us without money? Your plan gives us no revenue. No! but it does; for it secures to the subject the power of refusal, the first of all revenues. Experience is a cheat, and fact a liar, if this power in the subject of proportioning his grant, or of not granting at all, has not been found the richest mine of revenue ever discovered by the skill or by the fortune of man. It does not indeed vote you 152,750*l*. 11*s*. 2¾*d*., nor any other paltry limited sum; but it gives the strong box itself, the fund, the bank — from whence only revenues can arise amongst a people sensible of freedom. *Posita luditur arca*.[29] Cannot you, in England — cannot you, at this time of day — cannot you, a House of Commons, trust to the principle which has raised so mighty a revenue, and accumulated a debt of near 140,000,000*l*. in this country? Is this principle to be true in England, and false

---

29. With one's whole cash-box at stake — an allusion to excesses in gambling.

everywhere else? Is it not true in Ireland? Has it not hitherto been true in the Colonies? Why should you presume that, in any country, a body duly constituted for any function will neglect to perform its duty and abdicate its trust? Such a presumption would go against all governments in all modes. But, in truth, this dread of penury of supply from a free assembly has no foundation in nature; for first, observe that, besides the desire which all men have naturally of supporting the honor of their own government, that sense of dignity and that security to property which ever attends freedom has a tendency to increase the stock of the free community. Most may be taken where most is accumulated. And what is the soil or climate where experience has not uniformly proved that the voluntary flow of heaped-up plenty, bursting from the weight of its own rich luxuriance, has ever run with a more copious stream of revenue than could be squeezed from the dry husks of oppressed indigence by the straining of all the politic machinery in the world?

Next, we know that parties must ever exist in a free country. We know, too, that the emulations of such parties — their contradictions, their reciprocal necessities, their hopes, and their fears — must send them all in their turns to him that holds the balance of the State. The parties are the gamesters: but Government keeps the table, and is sure to be the winner in the end. When the game is played, I really think it is more to be feared that the people will be exhausted, than that government will not be supplied; whereas, whatever is got by acts of absolute power ill obeyed, because odious, or by contracts ill kept, because constrained, will be narrow, feeble, uncertain, and precarious.

"Ease would retract
Vows made in pain, as violent and void."

I, for one, protest against compounding our demands. I declare against compounding, for a poor limited sum, the immense, ever-growing, eternal debt which is due to generous government from protected freedom. And so may I speed in the great object I propose to you, as I think it would not only be an act of injustice, but would be the worst economy in the world, to compel the Colonies to a sum certain, either in the way of ransom or in the way of compulsory compact.

But to clear up my ideas on this subject: a revenue from America transmitted hither — do not delude yourselves — you never can receive it; no, not a shilling. We have experience that from remote countries it is not to be expected. If, when you attempted to extract revenue from Bengal, you were obliged to return in loan what you had taken in imposition, what can you expect from North America? For certainly, if ever there was a country qualified to produce wealth, it is India; or an institution fit for the transmission, it is the East India Company. America has none of these aptitudes. If America gives you taxable objects on which you lay your duties here, and gives you, at the same time, a surplus by a foreign sale of her commodities to pay the duties on these objects which you tax at home, she has performed her part to the British revenue. But with regard to her own internal establishments, she may, I doubt not she will, contribute in moderation. I say in moderation, for she ought not to be permitted to exhaust herself. She ought to be reserved to a war, the weight of which, with the enemies that we are most likely to have, must be considerable in her quarter of the globe. There she may serve you, and serve you essentially.

For that service — for all service, whether of revenue, trade, or empire — my trust is in her interest in the British Constitution. My hold of the Colonies is in the close affection which grows from common names, from kindred blood, from similar privileges, and equal protection. These are ties which, though light as air, are as strong as links of iron. Let the colonists always keep the idea of their civil rights associated with your government, — they will cling and grapple to you, and no force under heaven will be of power to tear them from their allegiance. But let it be once understood that your government may be one thing, and their privileges another, that these two things may exist without any mutual relation, the cement is gone — the cohesion is loosened — and everything hastens to decay and dissolution. As long as you have the wisdom to keep the sovereign authority of this country as the sanctuary of liberty, the sacred temple consecrated to our common faith, wherever the chosen race and sons of England worship freedom, they will turn their faces towards you. The more they multiply, the more friends you will have; the more ardently they love liberty, the more perfect will be their obedience. Slavery they can have anywhere — it is a weed that grows in every soil. They may have it from Spain;

they may have it from Prussia. But, until you become lost to all feeling of your true interest and your natural dignity, freedom they can have from none but you. This is the commodity of price of which you have the monopoly. This is the true Act of Navigation which binds to you the commerce of the Colonies, and through them secures to you the wealth of the world. Deny them this participation of freedom, and you break that sole bond which originally made, and must still preserve, the unity of the empire. Do not entertain so weak an imagination as that your registers and your bonds, your affidavits and your sufferances, your cockets[30] and your clearances, are what form the great securities of your commerce. Do not dream that your letters of office, and your instructions, and your suspending clauses are the things that hold together the great contexture of the mysterious whole. These things do not make your government. Dead instruments, passive tools as they are, it is the spirit of the English communion that gives all their life and efficacy to them. It is the spirit of the English Constitution which, infused through the mighty mass, pervades, feeds, unites, invigorates, vivi-

---

30. A document bearing the seal of the custom-house.

fies, every part of the empire, even down to the minutest member.

Is it not the same virtue which does everything for us here in England? Do you imagine, then, that it is the Land Tax Act which raises your revenue? that it is the annual vote in the committee of supply which gives you your army? or that it is the mutiny bill which inspires it with bravery and discipline? No! surely no! It is the love of the people; it is their attachment to their government, from the sense of the deep stake they have in such a glorious institution, which gives you your army and your navy, and infuses into both that liberal obedience without which your army would be a base rabble, and your navy nothing but rotten timber.

All this, I know well enough, will sound wild and chimerical to the profane herd of those vulgar and mechanical politicians who have no place among us; a sort of people who think that nothing exists but what is gross and material, and who, therefore, far from being qualified to be directors of the great movement of empire, are not fit to turn a wheel in the machine. But to men truly initiated and rightly taught, these rulings and master principles which, in the opinion of such men as I

have mentioned, have no substantial existence, are in truth everything, and all in all.
Magnanimity in politics is not seldom the
truest wisdom; and a great empire and little
minds go ill together. If we are conscious
of our station, and glow with zeal to fill our
places as becomes our situation and ourselves,
we ought to auspicate all our public proceedings on America with the old warning of the
church, *Sursum corda!* [31] We ought to elevate
our minds to the greatness of that trust to
which the order of Providence has called us.
By adverting to the dignity of this high calling
our ancestors have turned a savage wilderness
into a glorious empire, and have made the most
extensive and the only honorable conquests—
not by destroying, but by promoting the wealth,
the number, the happiness, of the human
race. Let us get an American revenue as we
have got an American empire. English privileges have made it all that it is; English privileges alone will make it all it can be.

In full confidence of this unalterable truth,
I now, *quod felix faustumque sit,* [32] lay the
first stone of the Temple of Peace; and I
move you —

---

31. Lift up your hearts—the Roman Catholic call to prayer.
32. May it be happy and of good omen.

"That the Colonies and Plantations of Great Britain in North America, consisting of fourteen separate governments, and containing two millions and upwards of free inhabitants, have not had the liberty and privilege of electing and sending any Knights and Burgesses, or others, to represent them in the High Court of Parliament."

Study of On Conciliation with America

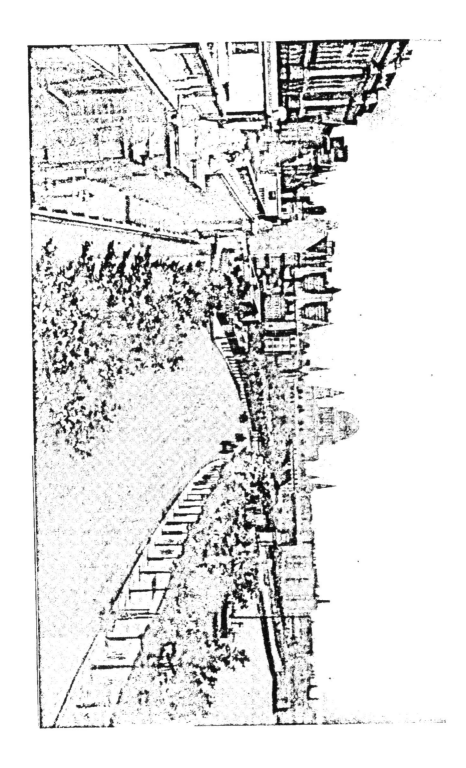

Studies

This oration is one of the finest examples of close and sustained logical argument that the English language offers us and it should be carefully studied. First with the idea of mastering its thought: Read it through from beginning to end rapidly, and with the idea of gaining a comprehensive knowledge of it in its entirety. Then go over it again more carefully, satisfying yourself that you have mastered the meaning of each sentence and that the chief points of the argument are fixed in your mind. Examine carefully the notes whenever you need their assistance, remembering that the dictionary is an indispensable adjunct to your work in literature. The notes are meant to assist you in finding what is not readily accessible to the ordinary reader.

To assist in the second reading, or in a third if it is necessary to read again, consult frequently the following outline, which will help to clarify the trend of thought.

Introduction. Opens the subject and clears the way by stating the two leading questions which the orator thinks should be decided :

Studies

1. Ought concessions to be made?
2. What should the concessions be?

Argument.   This presents

1. The condition of the colonists.
    1. The number of the colonists.
        (a) Present, very large.
        (b) Growing rapidly.
    2. Their commerce.
        (a) Extensive.
        (b) Phenomenal growth.
    3. Their agriculture—The New World feeds the Old.
    4. Fisheries—Their vessels are everywhere.

(Possibly more closely connected with a succeeding portion of the argument is the next section which offers to the use of force the objections that it is but temporary in its action, it is uncertain in its effect, it impairs the object sought, and experience has not justified it.)

II. The character of the colonists: A love of freedom is the predominating feature which marks and distinguishes them. Causes:
    1. Birth— descendants of Englishmen and so especially sensitive to taxation.
    2. Form of government— in a certain sense representative.
    3. Religion in northern colonies — Protestant.

266

4. Customs in the southern colonies — where slaves are held those who are free are especially proud and jealous of their freedom.

5. Education — Particularly the study of law.

6. Distance from the mother country — In large bodies the circulation must be less vigorous in the extremities.

III. Question: What shall be done?

(Here follows further explanation with allusions to pernicious experiments that have been made.)

There are three ways of proceeding:

1. To change the spirit by removing the cause. Plans that have been proposed and their difficulties:

(a) Make no further grants of land. This is neither prudent nor practicable because

(1) There are plenty of unsettled lands in private hands.

(2) People would occupy lands without grants.

(b) Impoverish the colonies — especially arrest their marine enterprises. But

(1) Discontent will increase with misery.

(2) They cannot falsify their pedigree.

(c) Change their religion, education, and
form of government. To accomplish this
  (1) The army would be ineffectual
  and chargeable to us.

(d) Enfranchise the slaves. But
  (1) Americans may arm servile
  hands.
  (2) May be suspicious of a nation
  that sanctions the slave traffic.
  (3) The ocean remains a barrier.

2. To prosecute the spirit as criminal. But
  (a) To prosecute an empire is impossible. Subordinate parts must
  have local privileges and immunities — imprudent to insist that
  if a single privilege is pleaded,
  authority is denied.
  (b) The judge cannot act impartially
  in a case when he is one of the
  parties.
  (c) Menaces cannot abate disorder.

3. To comply with the American spirit as
  necessary. This means
  (a) Grant them the boon they ask,
  representation in the Parliament
  that taxes them.

    (The *right* of taxation is not in-
    volved in this argument.)

(b) Admit the people of our colonies into an interest in the constitution. Reasons:

   (1) No danger of extension of demands.

   (2) Favorable precedents.

     (a) Ireland responded cheerfully in grants, but would not submit to taxation.

     (b) Wales was pacified by grants of constitutional liberties.

     (c) Chester demonstrated that freedom is the cure for anarchy.

     (d) Dover, a fourth example.

(c) Mark the legal competency of the colonial assemblies.

(Then follow in detail the six resolutions and their corollaries by which Burke hopes to bring about conciliation with the colonies. These resolutions having been discussed each by itself, he proceeds to dispose of some objections that had been raised to his plan, he examines and refutes the plan proposed by Lord North, compares it with his own plan.)

Conclusion. A strong plea for magnanimity.

The difficult thing is to follow a course of reasoning and to determine whether it is wholly logical; accordingly, after the argument in this oration has been carefully studied you should test each step to see if it meets your unprejudiced approval. If you had been a member of Parliament at the time would you have decided to vote with Burke for conciliation with America? If so, would you have done it because you were moved by his argument or because you were impressed by his own earnestness and sympathy with the colonists?

When the thought is fully your own, the whole oration should be read again and the parts compared in order to ascertain their relative merits. In so doing consider the following points:

I. Is the language clear so that you are not troubled by involved sentences and expressions of doubtful meaning? Do you find some passages more lucid than others?

II. Would his ideas make an impression upon the minds of his hearers? Are they forcibly expressed? Has he given them greater force by repetition and by varied expression? Does his oratory ever rise to a point where you would think his own feelings were involved? Can you imagine that he was ever deeply stirred by his interest in his subject? Did he ever make any direct appeal to the sympathies of his hearers?

III. Do you find any evidences of artistic finish? Has he tried to make his sentences sonorous and charming to the ear? Does he draw on his previous study for figures to beautify his sentences? Which characteristic prevails, clearness, force, or beauty?

Neither of the great orations you have just studied has been mastered until you are able to see the course of argument from beginning to end, until you have carefully weighed the proofs by which each step in the argument is established. You must not be caught by the fervid eloquence, the beauty of diction or the apparent logical sequence of ideas. You must be on guard to detect · fallacies in argument, conclusions that do not follow from the premises laid down, generalizations that should not be made from facts cited. When Burke cites the cases of Ireland, Wales, Chester, and Durham, does he prove his point? Could the revulsion in the condition of these provinces have been attributed to any other cause?

When Burke is speaking of the commerce of the colonies he refers to the fact that "this ground * * * has been trod * * * by a distinguished person at your bar," a gentleman whom he ranks as "one of the first literary characters of his age." This man was Richard Glover, a poet (1712–1785), who in 1761 was a member of Parliament and highly regarded for his scholarship, especially in Greek. But his was the age of Goldsmith, of Gibbon, of Adam Smith, of Dr. Johnson, and Boswell. To rank Glover as one of the first literary men of the time is grave exaggeration, for he possessed no power to make himself remembered. Find the passage and determine why Burke should so rate him. Was it because he really esteemed him so highly, was it to give increased value to any statements he might quote from Glover, or was he speaking ironically? Might such exaggerations tend to give too much weight to argument and carry conviction where it was not justified?

Comparing his speech with that of Webster in reply to Hayne, which do you think excels in logic? Which in clearness, in force, in beauty? Do you find in Burke such a fervid climax as that with which Webster closed his reply to Hayne? Do you find in either oration bright aphorisms, wise conclusions or moral reflections of a general nature which might be taken from their context and still be forcible and beautiful? From which oration can you select the more? As you look back over the two, which seems to you the better one, which would you prefer to have heard? If you had heard both, which would have pleased you the more, which would have been more stirring to your feelings, which the more convincing to your intellect?

Miscellaneous

Supplementary Readings

The two orations given are political in their nature and there are many others that are interesting reading. G. P. Putnam's Sons of New York publish a series of four small volumes called *American Orations* in which the speeches are arranged in chronological order so that a student may follow the history of his country in the orations its famous men have delivered. The first volume gives those of the colonial period and during the rise of the national spirit, the second and third relate to the antislavery struggle and secession, the fourth to the Civil war, reconstruction, free trade, and civil service reform.

The orations of Wendell Phillips are published in two rather larger volumes by Lee & Shepard of Boston. In the *First Series* are his antislavery speeches and among others in the *Second Series* are *The Lost Arts* and *The Scholar in a Republic,* two of the more famous.

A very fine collection is that of the orations of George William Curtis, edited by Charles Eliot Norton and published in three large volumes by Harper & Brothers of New York.

As a companion to *American Orations,* G. P. Putnam's Sons publish *British Orations,* a collection of the most famous political speeches of English orators. In an introduction to this set, Charles Kendall Adams says of the men whose speeches are given, "Eliot and Pym formulated the grievances against absolutism, a contemplation of which led to the revolution that established Anglican liberty on its present basis. Chatham, Mansfield, and Burke elaborated the principles which on the one hand drove the American colonies into independence and on the other enabled their independence to be won and secured."

Review Questions

1. Compare Webster and Burke in regard to their political positions and influence.

2. Which of the two speaks in the more figurative language ? Which is the easier to follow in his line of argument? Which the more entertaining to read ?

3. Compare the final paragraphs of *The Great Stone Face,* Lamb's *Dream Children,* Emerson's *Self-Reliance,* and Webster's *Reply to Hayne.*

4. Does the conclusion in all of these subserve the same purpose ? Is it in any case a direct appeal to the emotions ?

5. In what respect should the study of an oration differ from the study of an essay ?

6. Does the presence of such a person as Sir Roger de Coverley add to the interest of the essays in which he appears ? If so, in what way and for what reason ?

7. Which is the more readable, *Self-Reliance* or the *Reply to Hayne?* Why?

8. Find expository passages in the fiction of the first two Parts of this course.

9. Find descriptive prose in the two orations.

10. Compare Lincoln's *Gettysburg Address* with Bacon's *Nature in Men.* Can you see any points of similarity ? What difference do you notice ?

CPSIA information can be obtained
at www.ICGtesting.com
Printed in the USA
BVHW091245021118
531988BV00012B/1184/P